Twayne's United States Authors Series

Sylvia E. Bowman, *Editor*

INDIANA UNIVERSITY

Gore Vidal

GORE VIDAL

By RAY LEWIS WHITE

TUSAS 135

Twayne Publishers, Inc.   ::   New York

MANUFACTURED IN THE UNITED STATES OF AMERICA BY
UNITED PRINTING SERVICES, INC.
NEW HAVEN, CONN.

In Honor of
Lambert Davis

GORE VIDAL

by

RAY LEWIS WHITE

Gore Vidal is the first book about the writer's life and works. Although Vidal spent his youth among the famous men of Washington, D.C., his own biography has not before been told; nor have his ethical, political, and critical beliefs been discussed.

Using the author's private papers and his public statements, Ray Lewis White provides the biographical and the bibliographical data that are essential to appreciation of Vidal's ten novels and four plays, all of which Mr. White critically examines and evaluates. Mr. White's judgment of Gore Vidal's contribution to American letters will surely become a standard commentary on the achievement and the promise of a major contemporary writer.

Preface

TO WRITE the first critique of an author's work involves at once a special pleasure and a special responsibility. The pleasure derives from knowing that one is attempting to formulate ordered judgment where before perhaps only chaotic impression has prevailed. The responsibility comes from knowing that one's judgments may influence future appreciation of the writer's books. It may, therefore, be fortunate that first critiques, like first novels, are seldom classics; but good first critiques may call forth better second and third studies. I trust that *Gore Vidal* is such a book.

If great studies answer all questions about their subjects, my own work is more modest. I try in *Gore Vidal* to answer sharply defined questions: who is Gore Vidal? what does he believe? what has he written? and how valuable are his books? To provide as much information as possible about Gore Vidal, I discuss his background and his way of living, drawing many data from the author's private papers, to which I have enjoyed access. To outline what he believes, I quote at length from his published and unpublished statements on ethics, politics, and literature. To appraise his books, I allow the author to explain his own motives for writing each novel and play and also his opinion of their value; and then I place the works in literary traditions and in the Vidal canon.

Gore Vidal is organized thus: Chapter I outlines Vidal's biography and philosophy; Chapter II discusses three early novels, written in "the national manner"—*Williwaw, In a Yellow Wood,* and *The City and the Pillar;* Chapter III treats three experimental novels—*The Season of Comfort, A Search for the King,* and *Dark Green, Bright Red*—and the short stories in *A Thirsty Evil.* Chapter IV covers two "early but mature" novels—*The Judgment of Paris* and *Messiah;* Chapter V discusses four long dramas, with emphasis on *Visit to a Small Planet* and *The Best Man;* Chapter VI analyzes *Julian* and *Washington, D.C.,* Vidal's recent best-selling novels. Finally, Chapter VII presents several critical estimates of Gore Vidal's books and ends with my own statement of his accomplishment.

If *Gore Vidal* gives pleasure to its readers and in response causes them to read and enjoy Vidal's own books, my work will have been successful.

RAY LEWIS WHITE

Illinois State University
Normal, Illinois

Acknowledgments

First, I thank Gore Vidal for answering my many questions, giving me access to his personal papers, and letting me quote from unpublished material and published works for which he owns copyright.

Second, I am grateful to three libraries for extending to me their resources: The Newberry Library of Chicago, The State Historical Society of Wisconsin Library at Madison, and the D. H. Hill Library of North Carolina State University.

Third, I acknowledge my debt to the following individuals for aiding me in various professional capacities: John W. Aldridge, University of Michigan; Rodney Armstrong, Davis Library, The Phillips Exeter Academy; Josephine L. Harper, State Historical Society of Wisconsin Library; Robert E. Hawk; Walter Emil Kaegi, University of Chicago; Stebleton H. Nulle, Michigan State University; Agnes N. Tysse, University of Michigan Library; and Jay Williams, Little, Brown and Company, Inc.

Finally, I thank the following individuals and institutions for permission to quote from copyrighted material:

The Condé Nast Publications, Inc., for Eve Auchincloss and Nancy Lynch, "Disturber of the Peace: Gore Vidal," from *Mademoiselle*.

E. P. Dutton and Company, Inc., for Gore Vidal, *The City and the Pillar* (Copyright © 1948 by E. P. Dutton and Company, Inc.) and Gore Vidal, *The City and the Pillar Revised* (Copyright © 1965 by E. P. Dutton and Company, Inc.).

Farrar, Straus and Giroux, Inc., and the author for John W. Aldridge, *After the Lost Generation* (Copyright © 1951, 1958 by John W. Aldridge).

Grove Press, Inc., for Gore Vidal, *Romulus* (Copyright © 1966 by Gore Vidal).

Little, Brown and Company, Inc., for Gore Vidal, *The Best Man* (Copyright © 1960 by Gore Vidal); *The Judgment of Paris*

Contents

Chronology

1925   Eugene Luther (Gore) Vidal born, October 3, in West Point, New York, the only child of Eugene Luther Vidal and Nina Gore Vidal. Family moved to Washington, D.C.; attended elementary school there.

1935   Parents divorced. Lived intermittently with grandfather, Thomas Pryor Gore (Senator, Oklahoma).

1939   Toured England and Southern Europe. Studied at Château du Mont Cel, Seine-et-dis-è, France, June-September. Entered Los Alamos School, Los Alamos, New Mexico, in September.

1940   Left Los Alamos School in June. In September entered Phillips Exeter Academy, Exeter, New Hampshire.

1943   Graduated from Phillips Exeter Academy in June. Joined the United States Army, July 30. Attended Virginia Military Institute one term to study engineering.

1944   Appointed maritime warrant officer at Peterson Field, Colorado, October 24. Discharged as sergeant, November 7. Began writing *Williwaw*.

1945   Appointed first mate for the *F.S. 35*, Army Transport Service (Alaska), January 29. Treatments for arthritis until 1946. Completed *Williwaw*.

1946   Separated from armed services, February 15. Worked as editor for E. P. Dutton and Company, Publishers. Published *Williwaw* in the spring.

1947   Lived in Antigua, Guatemala, writing *The Season of Comfort*. Published *In a Yellow Wood*.

1948   Toured Europe in spring and winter. Met Tennessee Williams, Paul Bowles, Christopher Isherwood. Visited André Gide and George Santayana. *The City and the Pillar*.

1949   Returned to Guatemala to finish *Dark Green, Bright Red*. In New Orleans in the winter writing short stories. *The Season of Comfort*.

1950   Bought "Edgewater" for permanent home, north of West Point, New York, in July. *A Search for the King* and *Dark Green, Bright Red*. Began lecturing to help pay for house.

1952   *The Judgment of Paris*, the first "Edgewater" novel.

1954   Began with "Dark Possession" in February almost two years of writing television drama. *Messiah*, the second "Edgewater" novel.

1955   Continued "five-year plan" to achieve financial security by "visiting" California to write film scripts.

1956   Toured Europe in spring. Visited London to write script for movie *I Accuse. A Thirsty Evil* and television plays.

1957   *Visit to a Small Planet* successful on Broadway and published.

1958   Visited London to write film script for *The Scapegoat*.

1959   Wrote script for movie version of Tennessee Williams' *Suddenly Last Summer*. Wrote drama reviews for *The Reporter* and started *Julian*.

1960   *The Best Man,* a Broadway success, published. Defeated in election for Congress in the twenty-ninth district of New York. Produced *On the March to the Sea* at Hyde Park, New York.

1961   Wrote several commentaries for *Esquire. On the March to the Sea* produced in Germany.

1962   Began *Washington, D.C. Romulus* produced on Broadway. Published *Three* and *Three Plays*.

1963   Toured Southern Europe and the Near East. Lived in Rome much of the year, completing *Julian* and revising *The City and the Pillar*.

1964   Conducted a "talk program" for a New York City television station to influence the congressional election. *Julian* a best seller. Rejected second chance to run for Congress.

1965   Lived in Europe, polishing film scripts for *Is Paris Burning?* and *The Night of the Generals.* Published revised versions of *The City and the Pillar, The Judgment of Paris,* and *Messiah.*

1966   Lived in Paris and Rome, finishing *Washington, D.C.* Published text of *Romulus.*

1967   Tenth novel, *Washington, D.C.,* published.

Gore Vidal

CHAPTER 1

A Civilized Man

I HAVE observed," wrote Mr. Spectator in 1711, "that a Reader seldom peruses a Book with Pleasure, 'till he knows whether the Writer of it be a black or a fair Man, of a mild or cholerick Disposition, Married or a Batchelor, with other Particulars of the like Nature, that conduce very much to the right Understanding of an Author."[1] Excessive reliance on judging a work of literature according to the relation it bears to an author's life produces the "author fallacy." Total disregard for relevant biographical data leads, on the other hand, to the more serious fallacy of the "new criticism"—the assumption that a work of literature must exist as a separate pearl, perfect or flawed in its accreted layers but never to be regarded as the product of a special animal living in special waters and secreting material of at least some value in response to specific stimuli. However, before one can honestly appreciate any particular book in an author's canon or, better, read bravely and chronologically through the author's complete works, it is wise for a critic to be moderately familiar with the manner in which the author has chosen to live, with the forces that have governed his choices, and with his timely reflections on his own life and writing.

In the case of Gore Vidal, knowing at least the general facts of the writer's life and the relation of these data to his thought is imperative. Almost any moderately well-educated American or Englishman has wondered at this strange name, which he has seen recurrently on the spines of books, the programs of plays, the credit lines of movies, and in the social and literary columns of newspapers and magazines. He has been confused over publicity given *The City and the Pillar*,[2] he has heard of Vidal's political activities, and he has probably bought and read a copy of *Julian*. He has doubtless asked himself whether one man could deserve such publicity; then he has become aware that he actually knows nothing about the life of the author. This disturbing knowledge is due less to Vidal's having concealed his background and activities than to his never having cultivated very actively any popular public image. But Gore Vidal's biography is not disappointingly slim; he has not, in imitation of Horace or Gustave Flaubert, "just stayed home and written."

I A Fair Youth

Gore Vidal's father, Eugene Luther Vidal—born in Madison, South Dakota, in 1895—was one of the football heroes of his home town and later of the University of South Dakota, where he studied civil engineering. The Vidal family traces its history back to sixteenth-century Italy; Vidals came to Venice with Charles V and settled as chemists along the canals. They later became subjects of Austria, and in 1848 members of the family came to America.[3] Gene Vidal, because of his degree in engineering and his athletic prowess, obtained a commission to attend the United States Military Academy at West Point, New York, where he studied aeronautics and continued to be called a great football player. Graduated from West Point in 1918, Vidal was hired by that school to teach aeronautics and football.

Gene Vidal's marriage to Nina Gore, which took place in 1921, must have been a prominent social occasion—the football hero marrying the Washington socialite. The Gore family, of Anglo-Irish descent, came to America in the seventeenth century, settled in Mississippi, and then sent pioneers westward. Nina Gore, born in Lawton, Oklahoma, in 1903, was the daughter of Thomas Pryor Gore (1870-1949), Oklahoma's first United States Senator (1907-1921, 1931-1937). Nina and her husband lived at West Point until their only child, named for the father, was born October 3, 1925, at the Cadet Hospital.

Within a year of the birth of his son, Gene Vidal resigned his position at West Point and moved his family to Washington, D.C., to live with Senator Gore. In 1928, Vidal began working with aeronautics firms; and eventually he established his own home and his own aircraft company, a forerunner of Eastern Airlines. However, Vidal's marriage, which was never happy, ended in divorce in 1935. Some of his marital difficulties may have arisen over political matters: Senator Gore resisted strongly the New Deal social measures of President Franklin D. Roosevelt, but Gene Vidal faithfully served the President as a director of aeronautics in the Department of Commerce (1933-1937).

Young Eugene Luther Vidal had begun living with his grandfather, Senator Gore, when his parents had first experienced the frequent "crucial moments" that in 1935 ended their marriage of fourteen years. Senator Gore owned a fine home in Rock Creek Park, D.C., and the attic library of that home became the first center of his grandson's life. The senator, himself blind, encouraged Gene to read voraciously: ". . . I read him Constitutional History and British common law mostly; for pleasure we had Brann's *The Iconoclast* and the Victorian poets. In his attic . . . there were seven or eight thousand books. The first I could read by myself was called *The Duck and the Kangaroo*. My favorites were Lane's *Arabian Nights* and a nineteenth-century *Stories from Livy*."[4]

When not with his grandfather, Gene Vidal attended various schools in Washington, but by 1936 he was studying at St. Alban's School and living at the Auchincloss estate, "Merrywood," near McLean, Virginia. Nina Gore Vidal had married Hugh D. Auchincloss, a wealthy investment banker, soon after her divorce in 1935. Living at "Merrywood" was pleasant for the young boy, who was very proud of meeting the great and the near-great of American political society; but Vidal now views these years more wisely: "We were brought up quite removed from real life. By that I mean the Depression and what the family would have termed 'disagreeable' people. It was a world of the rich and the powerful who were able to keep unpleasant things far from them."[5]

At the age of fourteen, he had completed his work at St. Alban's and was to attend Los Alamos School in the autumn of 1939. In the summer of that year, accompanied by five schoolmates and two masters from St. Alban's, Vidal traveled for the first time to Europe. After studying French at Josey-en-Josas, Château du Mont Cel, Seine-et-dis-è, the group toured Rome, where, Vidal recalls, he was very much impressed at seeing Benito Mussolini. In returning to the United States, he first experienced the war which he would later be a part of: "The border between France and Italy was shut at the end of August, but we managed to get through. In London I stood in front of Downing Street as Neville Chamberlain departed for the House to report that war was at hand. The actual declaration found us in Liverpool, boarding the *Antonia,* a sister ship to the *Athenia* which was sunk either the day before or the day after we embarked. [I] was in history, and delighted."[6]

The 1939-1940 school year at Los Alamos was unpleasant for Vidal, but in the fall of 1940 he began the three years at Phillips Exeter Academy, Exeter, New Hampshire, which he recalls as "among the happiest of [his] life."[7] At Exeter, the young man was for the first time completely free of the family problems that had soured his childhood. The Exeter years saw the first serious writing by Vidal; at fifteen, he wrote perhaps one-hundred pages of a novel about Mussolini, his mistresses, and spies, obviously based on the 1939 tour. In 1943, he adopted his mother's family name as his own first name, and as Gore Vidal he contributed to and helped edit *The Phillips Exeter Review.*

Vidal's juvenile poetry, best left undiscussed, is of quite resolute meter and didacticism; but in three published short stories the young man showed at least competent adolescent imagination. "The Bride Wore a Business Suit"[8] concerns the marriage of a Phillips Exeter boy to a local girl; they are, respectively, fourteen and fifteen years old. "Mostly About Geoffrey"[9] pretends to be a werewolf story written on toilet paper. "New Year's Eve"[10] tells sadly of the brief desire of an officer's wife for a young lieutenant. As this story intimates, the United States was by 1943 at war.

II War and Work

Entering World War II in 1941, the United States may have expected to win an easy victory. However, it soon became apparent that conducting war on three fronts—the Pacific, Africa, and Europe—might delay total victory for many years. By 1943, sensible observers could have predicted an end to the war by 1953, while more optimistic men might have suggested 1948 as the first possible year of peace. In this dark time, on July 30, 1943, only a few weeks after having been graduated from preparatory school at seventeen, Gore Vidal joined the Enlisted Reserve Corps of the United States Army.

The army, needing engineers at the time, sent Vidal to study engineering at Virginia Military Institute, Lexington, Virginia. He spent one term there writing on another novel; he proved to be less than satisfactory material for an engineer and was sent as a private into the Army Air Corps. Stationed at Peterson Field, Colorado, Vidal tired of the duties of clerking for a head-quarters company: "I was confident that not only was this war never going to end but that I was going to spend the rest of my life putting colored pins in maps. I determined to get into the war, or at least out of that map room. Let me quickly say that I had no desire to be a hero. All I wanted was to be a writer and I felt that I could best become one by remaining alive, but be-tween risking my life and enduring the boredom of that map room, I was willing to choose the former."[11]

At eighteen, he was too young to be appointed to Officers' Candidate School; and his vision was too imperfect to allow him to become a pilot. By chance, he learned that the Army Trans-portation Corps needed maritime officers: "Grimly I memorized a book on navigation. I studied everything to do with the sea. I took an examination. I passed it."[12] On October 24, 1944, Gore Vidal, nineteen, was appointed Maritime Warrant Officer (junior grade) at Patterson Field.

Passing this examination helped him escape from the map room in Colorado, but it did little to assure him action in the great battles of World War II, for he was assigned immediately to the Army Transport Corps on the Aleutian island of Umnak. On January 1, 1945, he became first mate on *Freight Ship 35* of the Alaskan Harbor Craft Detachment. "I still have nightmares of that time," he recalls. "It is one thing to pass examinations; it is another to put into practice what one knows only in theory. I had never worked on a ship in any way before and now I was a mate. The skipper was not much older than I and he had been to sea all his life. Luckily, he was amiable and helpful. The crew was tolerant, and I survived the winter of 1944-45. And everyone else survived: I managed not to wreck the ship."[13]

On the freight ship Vidal began his fourth attempt at writing a novel: ". . . making a regular run between Chernowski Bay and Dutch Harbor, in December, 1944, I wrote half of *Williwaw* in pencil in a gray ledger marked *Accounts;* then for the fourth time I gave up, convinced I couldn't finish anything."[14] With less than two chapters of *Williwaw* written, Vidal had to leave

Alaska, for he had contracted rheumatoid arthritis from living in the inhospitable climate. On March 9, 1945, he was shipped for hospital treatment to Fort Richardson, Alabama; then, having been moved to Birmingham General Hospital, Van Nuys, California, Vidal wrote another chapter of the novel. Again, however, he abandoned the work, this time because of arthritis in his hand.

To have the arthritis treated in a proper climate, Vidal received a limited-duty assignment to Camp Gordon Johnson in Florida. There he finished *Williwaw:* "One night while on duty as Officer of the Day, sitting alone in regimental headquarters, I listened to weather reports: a hurricane was on its way up the Gulf, heading toward us. Properly keyed up, surrounded by typewriters in a deserted headquarters, I began to write again. In a few weeks the book was finished."[15]

In October, 1945, after World War II had drawn to an earlier close than Americans had expected, Vidal was stationed at Mitchell Field, New York. Instead of working on the history of Mitchell Field that he had been assigned to write, he started another novel, *In a Yellow Wood.* Therefore, unlike most soldiers who plan to write novels "when the war's over," Gore Vidal, when he was separated from the armed services on February 15, 1946, had written two novels and needed only a job and a venturesome publisher.

Vidal met both needs at once by working as an editor for the New York publishing firm of E. P. Dutton and Company, which had agreed to publish *Williwaw* in April, 1946. When the book appeared, public notice of it was so favorable that he immediately quit his editorial duties because he "couldn't stand going to an office. I have never," he adds, "gone to an office since."[16]

By early 1947, Vidal was living in his own first home—a renovated sixteenth-century monastery near Antigua, Guatemala. Living in Central America was for Vidal more a matter of economic necessity than personal preference: his small supply of United States dollars was far more valuable in Guatemala than in New York City. In 1947, Dutton published Vidal's second novel, *In a Yellow Wood*, which dramatized the young author's dislike for sitting at office desks—in the army or in a New York publishing house.

The City and the Pillar, published in 1948, brought the author questionable fame and considerable fortune. This novel, which deals with homosexuality, was written in 1946 when Vidal was twenty-one; but Dutton delayed publication so long that other, "inferior" novels on the subject had lessened the potential impact of the work and thereby created suspicion among reviewers.

In early 1948, while visiting Europe for the first time since 1939, Vidal met several men who were to influence him and remain close friends—Tennessee Williams, Paul Bowles, Christopher Isherwood, André Gide, and George Santayana. Williams "adopted" the writer and took him on a tour by jeep through Italy, where Vidal was deeply impressed at meeting Santayana, who received the young American in his hospital room:

> We got on well; he was tolerant; he would answer my questions, but he never asked me a personal question and I'm not sure if he ever bothered to learn my name. But this was as it should be: he was eighty-five and I was twenty-three. He was the master; I was the pupil. When it came time for me to leave Rome, I said good-by to him. . . . At the door to the hospital we shook hands. Then, as I was halfway through the door, he said, "I think you will have a happy life." I stopped and turned, not knowing what to say. He gave me a mischievous smile and added: "Because you lack superstition." We parted and I never saw him again. But I often thought of what he said. I took it as a benediction laid on with the left hand, but secretly I have hoped it was a prophecy. So far it has proved true.[17]

In 1949, Vidal published *The Season of Comfort*, a disguised autobiography of his childhood, and returned to Guatemala to complete *Dark Green, Bright Red*, a tale of political revolution that fully exploited his experiences in Central America. He seemed to be enjoying great social and financial success, but the financial part of his success was precarious.

The year 1950 was crucial in Vidal's life: ". . . I published two novels: *A Search for the King* which had good reviews and no sales, and *Dark Green, Bright Red* which had bad notices and no sales—and optimistically bought the house at Barrytown on the Hudson River where I still live; I went broke; wrote in an absolute explosion of delight *The Judgment of Paris*, a picaresque which is my best book."[18] The house at Barrytown, called "Edgewater," was still part of the John Jay Chapman estate in Dutchess County, New York—an area of various Roosevelts, Vanderbilts, and Livingstons. Built in 1820, "Edgewater" had not been lived in since 1907. Vidal bought the house, just north of his birthplace at West Point, eleven acres of land, and a small island in the Hudson River for sixteen thousand dollars—a great real-estate bargain financed on borrowed money. "Edgewater" was Vidal's first real home:

> It's a retreat—in the religious, not the military sense. It's a place where I work. I was moved around so much as a child that, as soon as I was able, I wanted a place I could always come back to. It represents a kind of permanence. I've never had any sense of permanence about being alive . . . but I have a semblance of it with this house. . . . [In the city] I have a sense of being devoured. Each person you see takes a bite out of you, and at the end there's nothing left to take home. And after awhile you get numb and then callous and then perhaps rebellious. So you have to keep some solitude, just to sit and moon, or work, or whatever. It's amazing what you then find is going on in your head that you weren't aware of.[19]

To support himself and to make his mansion habitable, Vidal tried unsuccessfully to have his books made into movies; he also failed to sell dramatizations of his own works for television use, and he made very little money from two new novels—*The Judgment of Paris* (1952) and *Messiah* (1954). Although he was tenuously connected with his father's fiberglas products company and although he received annually fifteen hundred dollars from the estate of his stepfather, Hugh Auchincloss, Vidal was by 1952 living on borrowed money and on income from lectures. The lecturing paid well because Vidal had for several years been hailed, in both admiration and envy, as "the brilliant young author of six novels in five years"; but talking to audiences at colleges and ladies' clubs proved to be such a chilling experience that by 1954 Vidal had to find some other way of making money that would use his talent for writing without making it impossible for him to write as he pleased.

III *A Plan for Piracy*

The purchase of "Edgewater" ultimately led Vidal to abandon the "solitary life" of the novelist; *Messiah*, which appeared in 1954, was his last novel for a decade. He became a writer "for hire," although writing for money has never been especially frowned upon in America: "Survival was now a desperate matter. So I hit upon a kind of five-year plan: an all-out raid upon television, which could make me enough money to live the rest of my life. It's been a fascinating, wearying experience . . . barring the unexpected I am, in a modest way, financially set for life. If one has the stamina, there is a lot to be said for piracy."[20]

The treasure ship which he boarded in 1954 was that promising but brief flowering of television drama in the mid-1950's. Already the years 1953-1957 are called the "Golden Age" of American television—a time of superb scriptwriters, inspired directors, and great actors. With *Dark Possession,*[21] produced by the Columbia Broadcasting System on February 15, 1954, Vidal began the one and one-half years of working for television during which he wrote at least thirty scripts for such programs as "Omnibus," "Philco Playhouse," "Studio One," and "Suspense." The success of Vidal's best original plays—*Visit to a Small Planet*[22] and *The Death of Billy the Kid*[23]—and of his dramatic adaptations of short stories—William Faulkner's "Smoke"[24] and "Barn Burning"[25] and Henry James's "The Turn of the Screw"[26]—as well as the outstanding television plays which he collected in 1956,[27] prompted him to predict that a new renaissance of interest in good drama might engulf the millions of television viewers in the United States:

> A cynic might say that out of 1,400 plays a year there are bound to be a few good ones, the law of averages obtaining. Actually, what has happened is that the need for material of any kind to decorate the buzzing air is so great that the first requisite of a renaissance does now exist: An audience is waiting, an invisible passive audience, true, wired though they are for response by the various survey agencies, but still it is a real audience with a huge appetite for plays—and art, traditionally, comes best when it is needed.[28]

Apparently, Vidal overestimated the cultural appetite of the American public, which has, of course, substituted television watching for book reading; for, by 1962, the potential for a drama renaissance had died: "By the end of the 1950's, original drama had largely vanished from the air. Nor does it show any immediate sign of reviving. The advertisers make more money with junk; and since the right to exploit others in the interest of making money is the only right the average American would lay down his life for, there will be little change in television."[29]

This decline in the fortunes of television drama came just when Vidal's own scripts were being more often rejected and performances of his plays more severely criticized than before; he was perhaps growing tired of this particular form of writing for hire. Fortunately, even more lucrative entertainment media were ready to buy Vidal's dramatic talents—the commercial theater and the Hollywood movie companies.

Two of Vidal's plays have been extremely popular and both financially and critically successful. The first, *Visit to a Small Planet*, expanded from his most admired television drama of the same name, opened at the Booth Theatre in New York City on February 7, 1957, where it played for three hundred and eighty-eight performances. The second, *The Best Man*, opened at the Morosco Theater on March 31, 1960, and played for five hundred and twenty performances in New York City. *Romulus*, adapted from Friedrich Duerrenmatt's *Romulus der Grosse*, beginning on January 10, 1962, played for only seventy performances at the Music Box Theatre in New York.

The failure of *Romulus* could not have worried Vidal very seriously. Although his original "five-year plan" had ended in 1958, the habit of establishing financial security prompted him to accept undeniably generous salaries for writing movie scripts. He has since the mid-1950's worked on (seldom completely writing) scripts for the following movies: *The Catered Affair, I Accuse, The Scapegoat, Ben Hur, Suddenly Last Summer, Is Paris Burning?*, and *The Night of the Generals*. Vidal likes to "come in on a movie after somebody has already written a script and everyone's desperate because they have to start shooting on a certain date which means that it isn't going to take too much time to fix."[30] To criticism that such work is unworthy of a serious writer, Vidal replies with more sense than indifference:

> Unfortunately, one has to earn a living. For me it was less compromising to write for films than to teach, or review other people's books. Or journalism. Yet there is a destructive element in writing for hire and it is, simply, indifference: a man's defense when he believes or is made to believe that he is misusing his talent (and the public which was indifferent to the talent itself

is usually eager to point out its misuse). The sullen response—
and especially if he is successful in a worldly way—is indifference.
And it must be fought against in the dark hours for indifference
is death to the artist. Somewhere in that is a particular American
tragedy.[31]

IV *Away from Home*

By 1960, Gore Vidal had become more a "public figure" than
a secluded novelist. Writing scripts for television, Broadway, and
Hollywood had forced him to work with the great numbers of
people necessary to such media.[32] His fortune made, the writer
found irresistible an invitation to enter the world in which he had
spent his youth—politics. Vidal's grandfather, Senator Gore, was,
of course, still remembered in Washington, D.C.; but Vidal had
another political connection worthy of notice: he was tenuously
related to the family of John F. Kennedy, then campaigning as
the Democratic candidate for President of the United States.[33]
Having lived in Dutchess County, New York, for ten years, Vidal
was moderately familiar with local conditions; he accepted an
invitation from the Democratic party to run for Congress from
the twenty-ninth district of New York.

Vidal first thought of running for Congress when he debated
the desirability of capital punishment with a local judge. His
conviction for abolishing capital punishment, argued so per-
suasively in a strongly conservative area of New York, made him
attractive to local Democrats and Liberals, who hoped for a
political victory in the elections in November, 1960.[34] The Re-
publican candidate, J. Ernest Wharton, had been in the House
of Representatives for many years; and, in 1958, he had won the
congressional election with a two-to-one majority of votes.

Gore Vidal, thirty-five and wealthy, ran an enthusiastic campaign against Wharton, who was sixty-one and less than na-
tionally prominent. He opened his campaign by announcing "the
key question of the age . . . 'How much freedom do we really
want?' "[35] He admitted that his liberal friends found his favoring
amelioristic reforms while protecting individual freedom not
"liberal" enough: "In actual fact, I have always been a conservative cross borne sadly by liberal friends. I began life as an absolute monarchist, on condition of course that *I* be that monarch.
At about fifteen, I shifted reluctantly to the idea of constitutional

monarchy, privately deploring the fact that George Washington had not become king. By seventeen, I had got around to the American Constitution and, for all its flaws, I have yet to see a better alternative to our form of government."[36]

The actual issues of the New York campaign have not survived in print—if they were ever clearly stated. But Vidal, calling himself a "correctionist" ("If something is wrong in society, it must be fixed. At least one should try to fix it."[37]), has stated his central political belief:

> I vote No to "perfection," and Yes to change and survival. Most of us spend too much time solving international problems at cocktail parties, rather than dealing with those things which we might affect and change, the tying up of the loose ends in our own society. There are many of them, ranging from the abolition of capital punishment to school integration. On either of those great matters any citizen can be usefully engaged. He can also be useful in social and moral legislation, where there is much work to be done. As for civil liberties, anyone who is not vigilant may one day find himself living, if not in a police state, at least in a police city.[38]

Had Vidal won in the election, he would have been the first professional writer to sit in Congress. He did reduce his opponent's majority to its lowest level until 1960, but he lost the election: "It is a chastening experience to find that after a year's steady campaigning in a district of 400,000 people, a large majority will go to the polls not knowing the name either of their Congressman or of his challenger. They will vote the party they have always voted."[39]

Chastened by his defeat, Vidal unfortunately rejected an invitation to run again in the same district in 1964; in the overwhelmingly Democratic victories throughout the nation, he should have won, as did the Democratic candidate in Vidal's district. That opportunity missed, but apparently not much regretted, Vidal retains his qualified confidence in this nation's political system: "American society has many virtues which we should never underestimate. By fits and starts, we are attaining a civilization and, barring military accident, we shall certainly attain one before the Soviets. 'Be the First into Civilization!' Now *there's* a slogan for the two competitors."[40]

Temporarily abandoning politics after 1960, Vidal retired to Europe to write again. In 1963, he finished *Julian,* his first novel in almost ten years; the book had an amazing public success. The popularity of *Julian* in 1964 apparently prompted him to rewrite three of his early novels for republication in 1965. The revisions of *The City and the Pillar, The Judgment of Paris* and *Messiah* were Vidal's attempt at the age of forty to judge his past work and to improve the best of it:

> Putting to one side the lesson of [Henry James], the revision of books once published is not a common practice among American novelists, if only because very few of our writers are given the chance (no second acts in American lives, as they say). Also American writers for the last 50 years have tended to be subjective and romantic. A book is torn from its author's flesh and flung at the reader, as if to say: Is this book not a part of me? and am not I, like God, in all that I do? The thought of making an old text better would not occur to a romantic writer, if only because one's second thoughts tend to be intellectual rather than emotional . . . and why would anyone want to alter the feelings of an early self?[41]

The revisions, although regarded with suspicion,[42] did seem clearly to invite examination of the author's canon and of his "thought." Except for his own opinions of his work, that thought is less than revolutionary.

V *On the Unabsolute*

Gore Vidal's beliefs on large subjects other than writing are so much a part of the *Zeitgeist* that it is difficult to call them original or very profound. They have, nevertheless, grown from his own background and from his never having belonged to any of the various American "establishments" that demand allegiance rather than thought. Thus, about the institution of marriage Vidal can say:

> Evidence does seem to indicate that since a third of American marriages end in divorce, at least a third of our married population has no talent for marriage. Instead of denouncing those who find monogamy or togetherness or the raising of children difficult and unrewarding work, it might be more worthwhile to

re-examine the whole moral, legal, and economic basis of marriage and the family. Those who enjoy it and do it well should certainly be encouraged and admired. Those who have no gift for it should find other ways of fulfilling themselves.[43]

Of course, marriage is more an economic than a biological state, and monogamy is not common in nature:

But the sad thing about the human race is that when something doesn't work we never think to ask if the institution is at fault; we assume instead there's something wrong with us, with men and women. So we try to alter ourselves at enormous expense—through psychiatry, prayer, popular writing—when the fault isn't in us but in a custom no longer useful. Our appetites are what they are, and as long as they are not destructive of others—physically, even perhaps morally—they are not the concern of the state. I should be very much surprised if the institution of marriage as we have known it will exist in a hundred years' time.[44]

On the subject of love, his attitude has, not surprisingly, changed since his youth. In the late 1940's, he could say: "We are responsible only to ourselves for what we feel just as others are responsible only to themselves for what they feel: the instant, however, when one man assumes some sort of responsibility for the feelings of another that instant demonstrates the highest degree of civilization and makes what could very easily be unbearable not only tolerable but at moments marvelous."[45] The mature Vidal regards love differently:

I don't know what future generations will think when they look back at our popular culture—they will think we were all absolutely out of our minds. Everything was love, love, love, and you have all these people who don't know quite what they're doing or talking about, but everything is going to be all right, they feel, when they have achieved this one more perfect union. As though it were an answer! Of course it isn't. It's only a very small part of life and it may be unachievable or undesirable. Love is like anything else, some people have more talent for it than others. Would we know what love was unless we'd been told?[46]

But, if love concerns people to an unreasonable extent, what might better concern them? To this question, Vidal replies: ". . . the great emotions, the great crises . . . anything to keep from surrendering to the idea that we are all victimized by the hugeness of society. Even if this is true, one should still attack the giant head-on; the alternative is paralysis or, worse, deliberate smallness. *We all know so much more than we write.* And why don't we write it? Because we are afraid of being thought stupid or wicked or . . . unlovable."[47]

Vidal has been more voluble on the subject of sex than on any other, especially on homosexuality, a theme of major importance in his writing:

> The obsessive concern with sexuality which informs most contemporary writing is not entirely the result of a wish *épater le bourgeois* but, more, the reflection of a serious battle between the society man has constructed so illogically and confusedly and the nature of the human being, which needs a considerably fuller expression sexually and emotionally than either the economics or morality of this time will permit. The sea is close. Two may find the interval between awareness and death more meaningful than one alone. Yet while ours is a society where mass murder and violence are perfectly ordinary and their expression in the most popular novels and comic books is accepted with aplomb, any love between two people which does not conform is attacked.[48]

Repressive moral legislation deeply concerns Vidal, who would

> change the sex laws in England and America. Or rather, remove the law entirely from sex, where it has no place. . . . Two thousand years of stern legislation cannot change biological fact. But of course we've done our best, and the results are all about us. In some ways, I was lucky to be brought up with no sense of sexual guilt. I was never told that masturbation was bad or that it was particularly wicked to go to bed with boys or girls. I also went into the army a month after my seventeenth [*sic*] birthday, and there was very little one didn't do. That established a promiscuous pattern which I'm sure has had its limiting side. But there have been compensations.[49]

To charges that he advocates moral anarchy or decadence, the author replies: "Contrary to current American opinion decadence is far more demonstrated in acts of violence, of deliberate sadism, of self-destruction, of perverse intensity than it is by any sort of irregular sex activity."[50] But he sees a humorous side to the subject of sex: ". . . perhaps the curious genius of our race

—unlike the non-sadistic, hedonistic Polynesians, for instance—is derived from the fact that by blocking most sexual drives, we have managed to keep ourselves in a state of irritability out of which have come the combustion engine and lyric poetry. Certainly German philosophy could only have come out of complete sexual frustration. No Greek could have written that way, no Polynesian could have conceived such things. But I'm not voting for further sexual frustration."[51]

Far more important, however, are Vidal's comments on writing. His attitude toward the role of the artist has remained remarkably consistent from the late 1940's to the present. When he was very young, Vidal defined his motives in writing as "a matter of compulsion, the urge to create, to establish a larger communication with the world, to be heard and understood, to establish some sort of order out of the amorphic shape of reality, to define the boundaries of all life."[52] The writer must appeal to an audience that identifies with him and his attitude toward his material: "Attitude then makes an artist and our judgment of an artist will always to a certain extent be governed by our ability to identify with his tone and his attitude. . . . It's rather the same thing as our reaction to a man's voice, to his face and, of course, to what he means to us that governs likes and dislikes in art as well as in life."[53]

The writer naturally falls into a tradition, "but ultimately a good novelist works outside his tradition; he creates a world separate from his contemporaries and separate from the actual one. It is his specific vision of reality, his sense of totality that in the end gives his work a tone and a particular accent which we recognize as style."[54] Writing must "have a vital relevancy to its own time and only in that relevancy does it have significance."[55] This relevancy is that of personal rather than mass communication:

> The writer can present the case and he can ask the questions and, for an instant, sometimes, he can give us a sense of sharing with him that most exquisite state of creativity, of perception where, out of all this flux and change which constitutes the universe, some order is suddenly made, a frame is found and a hierarchy is established. I think it's primarily to express that instant that an artist works and that is why one reads. I don't feel

that I'm being unduly chauvinistic when I say the chances of attaining that moment of sensibility are far more likely to occur in the reading of a poem or a novel than in a work of dialectic or a tract.[56]

The central statement of Vidal's early literary creed is that there should be "no fixed, dogmatic point of view in relation to which all actions must be judged and classified; rather the artist must create his own particular frame and the only fixed point in his work must be, of course, the point of awareness from which he observes the world."[57] This distrust of the absolute became the major tenet in his esthetic in the early 1950's. In 1952, he confessed:

I can hardly be a representative or popular twentieth-century writer, because never before has there been a century when the people have so desperately wanted certainty. I can't think why anyone should want it, but it is a fact and one at which I marvel. I accept the universe as impersonal, a great *is* which contains us all living or dead. I perhaps put too little value on human affairs, but I think not. If only because I am as partisan as the believers in my disbelief. You will say that if one accepts no absolutes how then can one, in the present instance, make any literary judgment? The answer is that one can, but only relatively, not ultimately.[58]

With no absolute values to govern literature, the writer has greater freedom:

The half of us which is still barbarian and superstitious laments the loss of the absolute, the personalized universe. The other half, aware of immensity, of the vastness of reality is moving out on its own and the expedition is painful but exciting and it is reflected in our art. Suddenly art assumes an altogether different meaning. It is not enough to describe characters and situations and judge them according to the prevalent laws concerning behavior: the challenge is infinitely larger: *to invent order where there is no order,* to give a sense of truth-saying while knowing that should there be an ultimate truth outside the form of time it is unknown to us, and will continue so. To realize that the order of the universe is, finally, inscrutable. . . .[59]

Vidal thus puts man without absolutes into historical and universal perspective:

> Our own age is one of man alone, but there are still cries, still struggles against our condition, against the knowledge that our works and days have value only in the human scale; and those who most clearly remember the secure authority of other times, the ordered universe, the immutable hierarchies, are the ones who most protest the black pit. While it is perfectly true that any instant in human history is one of transition, ours more than most seems to be marked by a startling variety of conflicting absolutes, none sufficiently great at this moment to impose itself upon the majority whose lives are acted out within an unhuman universe which some still prefer to fill with a vast manlike shadow containing stars, while others behold only a luminous dust which *is* stars, and us as well.[60]

The fact that man is neither creation's king nor the king's creature is the onus of modern literature: "For the writers there is no reality for man except in his relations with his own kind. Much of the stuff of earlier centuries—like fate, high tragedy, the interventions of *dei ex machina*—have been discarded as brave but out-worn devices, not applicable to a world where kings and commoners occupy the same sinking boat."[61]

The best known of Vidal's critical statements is his belief[62] *not* that the novel is dead but that "the large public is gone; the serious small public is not much interested in fiction, though on occasion a movie will get through to them. I'm not saying that one should not write novels. The thing is still worth doing for itself . . . at least there will always be moments of response to one's work to give a sense that the thing has happened, that what was written has made another mind aware."[63]

With its former public defected to television and movies, the novel

> is left only the best things: that exploration of the inner world's divisions and distinctions where no camera may follow, the private, the necessary pursuit of the whole which makes the novel, at its highest, the humane art. . . . To strike an optimistic note, if faintly, it may well be that, with unpopularity, the meretricious and the ordinary will desert entirely, leaving only the devoted

lashed to the mast. But now the tide is in. The course is set. The charts are explicit, for we are not the first to make the voyage out: the poets long ago preceded us into exile, and one can observe them up ahead, arms outstretched to greet the old enemy, their new companions at the austere edge of the known world.[64]

In spite of this public desertion of the serious writer, Vidal cares enough for his craft to entertain no thought of abandoning writing. He has so far written ten novels and four plays; he has lived and learned—and written:

To be demoralized by the withdrawal of public success . . . is to grant too easily a victory to the society one has attempted to criticize, affect, change, reform. It is clearly unreasonable to expect to be cherished by those one assaults. It is also childish, in the deepest sense of being a child, ever to expect justice. There is none beneath our moon. One can only hope not to be destroyed entirely by injustice and, to put it cynically, one can very often flourish through an injustice obtaining in one's favor. What matters finally is not the world's judgment of oneself but one's own judgment of the world. Any writer who lacks this final arrogance will not survive very long, especially in America.[65]

CHAPTER 2

In the National Manner

MEMBERS of each generation of American authors have had the choice, as they have begun writing, of adapting their work to fit at least one of the prevailing national tastes in literature or of trying to create an individual "personal style." Those young men who began publishing fiction at the end of World War II usually chose adaptation and wrote in what Gore Vidal calls "the national manner . . . a simple, calculated style, a bit simple-minded but useful. . . ."[1] This style resulted from a long tradition of colloquialism in American writing.

With political independence from England established, American writers soon desired to exhibit the products of their literary independence. However, early nineteenth-century attempts to write in the American instead of the English language were generally self-consciously humorous. Only after the American Civil War did the conscious, serious use of the American idiom become respectable—and that resulted mainly from one book, *Huckleberry Finn* (1884). The idiom and rhythm of this book, intellectualized by Henry James and analyzed by Gertrude Stein, became the stylistic mark of Sherwood Anderson. Anderson, of course, taught his style to Ernest Hemingway, and—through Hemingway—to the whole group of young men who imitated Hemingway in the 1940's. Gore Vidal, in his first three novels, wrote in this neo-Hemingway "national manner."

I Williwaw

World War II ended in August, 1945, but American writers continued to fight in their fiction the war which many of them had lived through on active duty. Involving as it did the total material and human resources of the nation, the war experience naturally brought about a seemingly insatiable demand for novels of wartime intrigue and battle. By 1967, Americans had published well over two hundred fictional accounts of World War II, many of them now forgotten but some already firmly established in the corpus of the literature of war.[2] Few Americans are unfamiliar with such popular World War II novels as John Horne Burns's *The Gallery* (1947), Irwin Shaw's *The Young Lions* (1948), Herman Wouk's *The Caine Mutiny* (1951), James Jones's *From Here to Eternity* (1951), and Joseph Heller's *Catch-22* (1955). Less famous than these, but worthwhile reading, Gore Vidal's *Williwaw*[3] occupies a distinctive place in American historical fiction.

Because "war is an irresistible subject, especially to a young man who has lived through one,"[4] Vidal based his first novel on his experiences, at nineteen, as a maritime warrant officer stationed at Chernowski Bay on the Aleutian island of Umnak. Thus removed from the scenes of actual fighting—Africa, Europe, and the Far East—*Williwaw* does not deal with the combat operations of World War II; instead, Vidal sees the war as a remote force that has thrown together a group of men in a difficult, inhospitable environment that aggravates their personal animosities and threatens their existence through natural disaster. The battles are not forgotten, but American soldiers fight personal conflicts and a dangerous sea.[5]

The revelation of human nature through descriptions of men facing disasters at sea is a literary convention as old as the story of Jonah and as new as the novels of Herman Melville and Joseph Conrad. Sea storms are perfect settings against which to delineate the personalities of men removed from the polite societies that check their tendencies toward more animalistic, possibly more "human," behavior. In using a storm at sea (or any great natural catastrophe) as the central situation in a novel, the writer must first describe his characters fully enough to enable the reader to accept the deeper revelations that the storm brings out. In *Williwaw*, Vidal solves this problem by dividing his narrative into three distinct sections: the events leading up to the "williwaw" and introductions of the characters, their backgrounds, personalities, and relation to one another; the storm itself and its effects on the men; and, finally, the aftermath of the storm, when a human disaster results on the ship.

"Williwaw," according to the author's prefatory note to his novel, is "the Indian word for a big wind peculiar to the Aleutian islands and the Alaskan coast. It is a strong wind that sweeps down from the mountains toward the sea" (7). Vidal's williwaw strikes a three-hundred-ton army freight-passenger ship as it moves among the Aleutian Islands from Andrefski Bay to Arunga. The voyage is begun in spite of adverse weather warnings because an army major must deliver official reports to his base in Arunga. Because no airplanes can attempt to make the trip, the small freighter is chosen for the dangerous crossing. Before the ship leaves Andrefski Bay, Vidal sets up in counterpoint the descriptions of seven main characters. Three of them are passengers for the journey; four, members of the freighter's crew.

Least important among the major characters of *Williwaw* is Lieutenant Hodges, "young and pink-faced" and "very solemn" (21). He is an agreeable cipher, an insignificant officer who behaves circumspectly because he wants a military career, a goal considered odd by his brighter associates. Chaplain O'Mahoney is a timid, nervous priest who fears sea-sickness: "He had been a monk in a Maryland monastery, and now, in the army, he acted as if he were playing a part in a bad dream" (34). Relying on his professional manners, he is awkwardly friendly while worrying about his blood pressure, indulging in vaguely hypocritical thoughts, and wishing he were back in his secluded monastery.

Major Barkison, the third and most thoroughly drawn passenger who braves the williwaw, shows the author's scarcely concealed disgust for the professional military officer, the small-minded egoist who plays army politics and is devoted only to his own prestige. A study in rank-consciousness, he "was a West Pointer and quietly proud of the fact. Though not much over thirty he was already bald. He had a Roman nose, pale blue eyes, and a firm but small chin. He looked like the Duke of Wellington. Knowing this, he hoped that someone might someday mention the resemblance; no one ever did, though" (19). Always anxious to be promoted, Barkison had in peacetime married his commander's daughter. He feebly tries to be agreeable to his inferiors in rank, but his pomposity and vanity incline him more toward striking classically military poses than to friendliness. On his insistence the ship leaves for Arunga during bad weather, for his "reports" must be delivered.

The skipper of the ship commandeered by Major Barkison is Evans, a young warrant officer obsessed with his profile (he tries continually to see it in mirrors) and with jingles that run through his head and cause him to doubt his sanity. Evans relies too heavily on liquor, for he is unhappy with his Alaska assignment and looks forward to commercial fishing after the war. Although he is competent at sea and deeply aware of his responsibility as skipper, he is unpopular with the crew and resentful of his first mate's assumed superiority. Evans fears the possible storm through which he must guide his passengers, but military red tape and rank override his warnings.

First mate on the freight-passenger ship is Martin; like Evans, he is a young warrant officer. In civilian life, Martin had been a stock-company actor, and his light humor and delight with learned words annoy the skipper. He assumes a "carefully studied collegiate manner although he has never been to a college" (28-29). Martin is popular with the crew; he is "dark and nearly handsome," and his voice is "deep, interesting and mocking"; but he knows nothing about being a first mate (29).

Even less individualized than Martin are the second mate, Bervick, and the chief engineer, Duval. As Evans is obsessed with his profile and Martin with his "superiority," these two men are obsessed with Olga, a Norwegian prostitute in Big Harbor, where the ship stops frequently on its usual runs. A New Orleans Frenchman, Duval is overbearing and much older than his skipper. Bervick is a technical sergeant, a professional army sailor who makes less money than Duval. He first enjoyed Olga's attractions free, but Duval's money had proved more interesting to the popular Olga than Bervick's love. Olga was not especially attractive; but, where women are scarce and men are together too much, strange things obsess people who have been at sea for a long time.

In writing *Williwaw*, Vidal wisely recognized the limitations of the young man creating his first novel: "Since my inexperience was obvious to everyone, it was all the more necessary for me to do the things I *could* do with a certain unobtrusive dispatch."[6] Vidal did not attempt, therefore, to write long passages of pro-

found character analysis. Instead, he presented outlines of his
seven main characters without giving them either fine shadings
or deep colors. The reader must piece together his idea of the
men who face the williwaw, drawing upon the author's occasional notations of their motives and their obsessions. There is
no direct entrance into their minds; they are identified by sketches
of their behavior that build up piece by piece to form composite
pictures of men at war with nature and with one another.

After a night at Big Harbor, where Duval and Bervick compete for Olga with money and affection, respectively, the small
ship continues its crossing from Andrefski Bay to Arunga. The
barometric reading lowers alarmingly; the proud chief engineer
taunts the second mate; and the other officers and the passengers
do nothing to stop their quarreling. Evans tries to escape the
impending williwaw by sheltering near Kulak Island, but the
storm forces the ship toward the rocks of the island. Evans and
Martin are unable to control the ship, which is almost certain
to destroy itself upon the island.

In this section, Vidal is at his best narrative ability. As the
ship rushes toward disaster, he describes through separate vi-
gnettes the effect of the williwaw on his characters. Duval and
the three passengers are caught in the salon by the force of the
one-hundred-mile-per-hour wind. Duval staggers to the engine
room to stop the ship's engines. Bervick, caught in the fo'c's'le,
makes his way to the deck in time to hear the mast break off.
Eight minutes after the williwaw strikes, the ship is miraculously
caught between two huge rocks near the island; in this position
it can weather the raging storm in comparative safety, although
Evans must look forward to docking his ship for extensive repairs.
In these few pages devoted to the williwaw itself, Vidal achieves
a tension in his writing that equals the best narratives of Ernest
Hemingway and Stephen Crane when they write of men help-
lessly facing destructive nature.

However, this storm scene is not the climax of *Williwaw*. For
as the storm subsides, the internal drama—the conflict between
Bervick and Duval—rises to new heights. These men, sent to
repair a broken ventilator covering, taunt each other because
of Olga until Bervick throws a hammer at Duval, who is sitting
on the ship's rail. Although Bervick, acting in a fit of anger, does
not intend to hurt Duval seriously, the engineer falls overboard.

When Bervick finds himself unable to do anything to aid the man drowning in the icy water, he fixes the ventilator and then discovers that no one knows of Duval's death. Only Lieutenant Hodges thought he had heard a splash while Bervick and Duval were on deck. No one on the ship is more than slightly sorry to know that the second mate is dead; no man cares deeply about another man's death, for the event does not seemingly affect his own life.

And this lack of personal interest in their companion's death on the part of the ship's crew and passengers is the point which Vidal tries to make in *Williwaw:* ". . . actions are important only to the degree *we* invest them with importance. My characters chose not to regard death as important; and it was not, to them."[7] The skipper and Lieutenant Hodges, if not the entire crew, mildly wonder whether Bervick was not somehow responsible for Duval's death; but they know that a charge against Bervick could not be proved. Eveyone takes the easy way out of the dilemma; and, upon reaching Arunga, each becomes involved in his individual concerns. The chaplain gossips with friends about his religious colleagues, Major Barkison is promoted to lieutenant colonel, Lieutenant Hodges meets a companionable lieutenant friend, and Evans declares Duval lost at sea. Ironically, Barkison, who reprimands Evans for having attempted such a dangerous crossing, shifts off his own role in putting the ship in danger. And, ironically, his "reports," delivered in Arunga, are merely his recommendation that Andrefsky Bay be shut down as an active military base.

Williwaw is thus a simple novel. The story depends on two situations—the storm at sea and the conflict over a woman—and the characters of the men involved are always suggested, never fully described. Much of the book is written in dialogue—terse, clipped, telegraphic. Vidal manages an unemotional tone that never reaches great feeling or grasps at profound meanings. There is no hero in *Williwaw;* there are only men who must cooperate to live through a common danger. Their experiences do nothing to coalesce their warmer sentiments; even the probable murder of a companion raises only a mild interest in their purposeless lives.

And this purposelessness is the author's final comment on humanity at war: the utter boredom, the mind-saving "insanity of obsessions," and the indifference of nature to man and of man to man reflect the futility of personal struggle and individual values. *Williwaw* is a cynical story, but no thoughtful young American who lived through World War II could have denied the truth of Vidal's cynicism. Having found and assumed this "truth," Gore Vidal could confidently say that, "with the finishing of this book, my life as a writer began."[8]

II In a Yellow Wood

While living through the experience of supporting and fighting a war, a nation's people naturally anticipate the enjoyment of post-war peace. The deprivation, sacrifice, and death that they had endured throughout the time of battle are expected to give way to stability, prosperity, and relaxation. Writers who made use of the national war experience for their novels turn to examining the problems of national and individual readjustment to non-military life. Thus the thousands of veterans returning to civilian life after World War II created and faced problems that were soon the bases of many novels, few of them remembered for long. The national interest in post-war adjustment resulted in such works as Niven Busch's *They Dream of Home* (1944), William Heyliger's *Home Is a One-Way Street* (1945), William Riley Burnett's *Tomorrow's Another Day* (1945), and Eleanor Mayo's *Turn Home* (1945).

Having treated his own wartime experiences in *Williwaw,* Vidal naturally based his second novel on an ex-soldier's problems in facing civilian life. Doubtless, the subject matter of *In a Yellow Wood*[9] was influenced by the author's memories of the routine, boring desk jobs that he had held, late in his army service, and by his work, in 1946, as an editor.

In a Yellow Wood is the story of Robert Holton, an ex-soldier who finds himself in the yellow wood of indecision made famous in Robert Frost's "The Road Not Taken": "Two roads diverged in a yellow wood,/ And sorry I could not travel both/ And be one traveler. . . ." But Vidal chooses to show the reader only one day in the life of his protagonist. In this twenty-four hours, during which Robert Holton must decide how he is to spend the rest of his life, he goes to work at a large brokerage house; attends a "society" reception; and awakens the next morning, his decision made. This simple framework allows Vidal to guide the reader through Holton's day, hour by hour; to introduce a rather large number of people who know or meet him; and to concentrate on *how* Robert Holton chooses the road to follow out of his yellow wood.

Robert Holton is not quite the ordinary young veteran returned from the war. He is drawn toward self-analysis, especially of the disturbing dreams which he can never quite remember. He is worried about his hairline, his physique, and his faint discontent with a very promising job as a clerk in the brokerage firm of Heywood and Golden, members of the New York Stock Exchange. Holton wakes in his hotel room, notices the yellow morning light of Indian summer, and dresses conservatively for his work since "it was a good idea not to be too vivid when you worked for a brokerage house" (10).

He has the illusion that he is the only occupant of his hotel; he yearns to dirty the white sand of the ash trays in the hall; and he carefully plans his day. Nothing important is to happen at the office; but he must attend a cocktail party late in the afternoon because Mrs. Raymond Stevanson, the hostess, was a friend of his mother and because "when one was starting out in the brokerage business contacts were important" (12). Holton remembers only momentarily his army experience; he longs now for a routine life with no surprises or jolts to disturb him. Beginning with the waitress who serves breakfast to Robert Holton, Vidal describes this young businessman as he is seen by various people during his day.

Marjorie Ventusa, a waitress at the restaurant where Holton regularly dines, is a too-blond, lovelorn woman who is silently infatuated with the young man who is always so careful to be polite to her—careful to say just the right thing in their bantering conversations. Marjorie, who inhabits a shabby dream-world that reflects her social entrapment in a shabby job, merely plays with the idea that Holton cares for her or really notices her at all; to her, this young man represents the "beautiful world" forever closed to women like her. Ironically, she imagines that Holton is thirty, four years above his actual age and seven years younger than she. Marjorie knows that people never get what they want; she resignedly faces the poverty and loneliness that such lucky people as Robert Holton never—she believes—have to endure.

Holton walks into the office of Heywood and Golden with
Caroline Lawson, secretary to Oliver L. Murphy, head of the
statistical department, in which Robert Holton is a clerk. Caroline,
a very pretty young woman, is not sure that Holton would be
deep enough or strong enough to "understand" her. Ironically,
there is almost nothing in Caroline to understand; she is vapid
and shallow, introverted and mildly worried about marrying and
about Holton's being promoted and forgetting her.

Vidal introduces three other characters from the brokerage
office, each of whom has a conception of how Robert Holton
fits into his own patterned life. Mr. Murphy worries about his
ulcer and little else. To him, exercising his small authority and
being agreeable to and noticed by his superiors are sufficient
satisfactions for his ego. Holton, a clerk in his office, is a rather
colorless face at a desk like other desks. To Dick Kuppleton,
however, Holton is a rival clerk after a fast promotion, depending
on his status as veteran to rise above Kuppleton, who must defer
to Holton in spite of his own seniority. Lawrence Heywood, co-
owner of the firm, is wealthy, cultured, and bored. About to
lose his third wife through divorce, Heywood cares little for his
business work; but he is lulled by the routine of stocks and bonds
and does not recognize his own captivity. He feels that he must
promote Robert Holton, whom he knows of through family con-
nections and whom he is to meet at the cocktail party later in
the day.

These three characters, and their fellow workers in the brokerage firm, go through the motions of their assigned work, enjoying
nothing and hating nothing, rather like the lines of figures they
deal with on their adding machines. Into the office, however,
there comes a new face to break the routine for at least Holton
and Caroline: Jim Trebling. Holton and Trebling had been constant companions in World War II, serving together in Italy.
Trebling visits Holton in the brokerage office, where, as a soldier,
he feels very much out of place. He causes Holton to remember
the women they knew in Italy, particularly a girl named Carla,
who had loved Holton but whom he scarcely recalls. Jim does
not like or really know the Robert Holton whom he now meets
—the colorless, empty, settled veteran who wants nothing more
than routine and conformity after the adventures of the war.
Trebling offers Holton the partnership they once planned—their

own business and a rather irresponsible, exciting life; but Holton wants no adventure now: he is tired of "moving about." Trebling leaves, after arranging a date with Caroline for that night, although to him Caroline is just another woman.

The second part of *In a Yellow Wood* describes the cocktail party which Robert Holton dutifully attends after his working day. Mrs. Raymond Stevanson, the hostess, gives the party because it is expected of her; the guests drink and gossip about trivia; and everyone hopes it will end soon. When Holton meets Mr. Heywood at the party, he is rather automatically promised a promotion from clerk to "customers' man" or agent; he meets George *Robert* Lewis, an effeminate, intellectual homosexual who is attracted to him; and he encounters Mrs. Carla Bankton, the woman he had made love to in Italy during World War II. Carla is married to a promising homosexual artist whom Lewis knows, but she has carried about with her the memory of Robert Holton, her first lover. Charming, cultured, and rich, Carla is delighted to meet her dream figure again; but she is shocked at his present colorless personality and his placid acceptance of a deadening existence. She loves Robert Holton enough to offer herself to him again, hoping that he still has the strength to break away with her to a life of adventure and love.

To demonstrate in the extreme the life which Carla offers Holton, Vidal has George *Robert* Lewis invite the couple to visit a Greenwich Village bar frequented by homosexual artists, writers, and intellectuals. Holton is mildly shocked by the bar, but Carla knows such places through her homosexual husband. She uses Lewis to show Holton what her husband is like and why she is willing to leave marriage for her first love—Holton. This bar scene is graphic: the patrons are cultured, intelligent, but lonely people escaping into talk of religion, philosophy, and love, while desperately looking for sympathetic partners. After seeing a sensual dance by the famed Hermes de Bianca, Holton and Carla leave the bar to walk through the crowded streets around Times Square.

Vidal brings his characters back together as Holton and Carla walk about. The waitress, Marjorie Ventusa, sees Robert with a beautiful woman and is jealous. She rejects a friendly pick-up offer from some lonesome man and escapes into a theater. Mr. Heywood, wishing he were young again and realizing his loneliness, goes to a show but leaves early to return to a secure if loveless home. Jim Trebling and Caroline go to a dance and look forward to their love later in the night. And, finally, Carla invites Holton to her hotel room.

Now Robert Holton is made to understand the choice he must make: he can recognize that he is not talented or cultured or "free" and stay in his patterned, stockbroker, routine existence; or he can let Carla love him and support him and become "free" by escaping with her to a bohemian, adventurous life. To Carla, love is *the* answer; but Holton does not know love or have the ability to see its importance. To Holton, who wants the "safe thing," the unimaginative routine with its security, going to Europe with Carla "just wouldn't be practical" (193).

The brief third section of *In a Yellow Wood* shows Robert Holton returning to his own hotel room after his hours of passion with Carla. He is uneasy and unable to sleep, for conversations he has heard during this very special day run through his mind. George *Robert* Lewis talks of religion and/or love as the answer to "the loss of a personal vision." Jim Trebling invites him to a drifting, easy life; but Holton has already "done the easiest thing": He is "entangled now for the rest of his life with Heywood and Golden; with them or another like them" (203). And Carla: he has carefully explained to her that he "must be within the pattern," and she "had let him go free to his chosen prison" (205).

Holton argues himself into a final decision. He barricades out loneliness, longing, and freedom: "He would become a decided person and he would cease to be changed by others. Robert Holton would become a successful broker working in an office. The decision was made and he felt secure at last. The words and thoughts that had been in his mind, troubling him, stopped abruptly" (207). Strangely, he can no longer come even close to remembering his dream from the previous night. Robert Holton sleeps, and the next morning he is promoted at the firm of Heywood and Golden.

In a Yellow Wood can, then, be considered a "problem novel." If it had been hoped that World War II would uproot society and destroy the staid dependence on "types"—on the stale custom and monotonous routine that had characterized American life —Vidal's novel demonstrates the inability of Americans to choose a new way of life, desirable as it might be. However, Robert Holton is never truly able to choose freedom; he had actually made his choice, consciously or not, during the war when he had longed for "no more moving about." Vidal is interested in showing the *way* Holton cannot make a decision to be intellectually and morally free. Dull, unimaginative, and colorless, Holton is not worthy of a life better than that of a plodding businessman. The old army buddy, the homosexual esthete, and the vibrant, amorous Italian woman deserve exciting lives. But the waitress, the secretary, the executive, and the young clerk deserve tedium. One feels that each had the chance to be free to search for fulfillment but that each was constitutionally unable to declare himself available for the insecurity of the search.

Stylistically, *In a Yellow Wood* continues to use the controlled naturalism of *Williwaw*. The language is plain, bluff, and detached; and again much of the novel is presented in dialogue. Vidal depends heavily on detail—the brokerage office, the cocktail party, the bar scene, the bedroom affair—to carry his narrative along. However, *In a Yellow Wood* shows a slightly more complex structure than that of *Williwaw*, and the handling of a larger cast of people with more complex motivations causes no technical problems for the author. Ironically, as the author must have intended, *In a Yellow Wood* leaves one feeling that there was no choice for Robert Holton at his crossroads in the social forest; he would never wonder again whether the other path might have been the better for him. To do so was *not* his chance.

III   The City and the Pillar

American writers will always be indebted to those novelists and dramatists who fought against the middle-class mores and puritan consciences that dominated the reading public in the early twentieth century. Such authors as Stephen Crane, Theodore Dreiser, Sinclair Lewis, and Sherwood Anderson had to struggle valiantly to be able to use as literary material adultery, promiscuity, prostitution, and incest. They eventually succeeded in shaping these and other previously forbidden subjects into widely read literature, but here they stopped. Only after World War II did many Americans have the courage to write seriously and to read understandingly about the one area of life seldom before explored—the world of the homosexual.[10]

Perhaps the experience of World War II did indeed lead to a reassessment of individual and national values; or perhaps the war taught Americans that only the relative morality of the individual—in the extreme, the homosexual—could be valid and important. Whatever the cause, American literature has since World War II incorporated such serious and popular works as Truman Capote's *Other Voices, Other Rooms* (1948), James Baldwin's *Giovanni's Room* (1956) and *Another Country* (1962), Tennessee Williams' *Cat on a Hot Tin Roof* (1955), Edward Albee's *The Zoo Story* (1960), and Hubert Selby, Jr.'s *Last Exit to Brooklyn* (1964). These novels and plays, critically and financially successful as they have been, owe much of their freedom in treating homosexuality frankly and honestly to the appearance of Gore Vidal's third novel, *The City and the Pillar*.[11]

"I was twenty-one when I wrote *The City and the Pillar*," recalls Vidal. "I was bored with playing it safe. I wanted to take risks, to try something no American had done before. I decided to examine the homosexual underworld . . . and in the process show the 'naturalness' of homosexual relations, as well as making the point that there is of course no such thing as a homosexual."[12] To accomplish these double aims of description and analysis, Vidal chose as his protagonist an "innocent," an ordinary, rather dull young man who moves more and more deeply from a surface naïveté into the varied strata of the world of the homosexual. As he does so, he reveals, if not understands, several truths about the nature of sex and love and finally demonstrates a sound philosophical position.

Structurally, *The City and the Pillar* utilizes a simple "frame device": one scene in the present serves to open and close the story, and the narrative presents chronologically the history of the main figure before the present scene. These memory chapters are the experiences of Jim Willard from the age of seventeen to twenty-five—roughly from 1936 to 1943. Using the text of Genesis 19:26, "But his wife looked back from behind him and she became a pillar of salt," the "City" part of the novel, with its overtones of biblical Sodom and Gomorrah, traces the innocent through a complex of relations; then the "Pillar of Salt" section reverses the track to lead to the scene of sadness in the present.

The character of Jim Willard is the author's attempt to shatter the American stereotype of the homosexual as an effeminate, socially undesirable interior decorator. Willard is an athlete, introduced as he sits alone in a bar, trying very hard to become drunk: "He looked about him but there was nothing interesting to see: only a bar in a city. He wasn't sure what city; only the bar had a certain relationship to him because there was no one else in the world except himself" (12). Willard is afraid of something: he is twenty-five years old, and he wants no memory at all. He rejects rather cruelly the offers of a friendly prostitute and continues drinking, "although, no matter how much he tried, he could not destroy the fear: he could only forget, for a while, how it began" (20).

The disaster responsible for Jim Willard's present anguish has its origins in his first experience of sexual fulfillment, at the age of seventeen, with a boyhood friend in Virginia. Jim, second of the Willard children, has an ordinary older sister and an unpleasant younger brother. Not especially handsome, sociable or intelligent, Jim by athletic prowess gives a basis to his friendship with Bob Ford, an eighteen-year-old being graduated from high school. In order to escape from his ill-tempered father and his weak-willed mother, Jim spends one last weekend with Bob at a deserted cabin outside town. Realizing that Bob must leave home to find work in New York, Jim dares for the first time to live his almost unconscious dream of sexual fulfillment with Bob. They act naturally, ecstatically, and guiltlessly; and then they part. This experience, described with restraint and sensitivity by Vidal, becomes the point in Willard's life that remains his ideal, his secret touchstone for measuring all later adventures.

Jim spends his eighteenth Christmas as a cabin boy on a small passenger ship, on a trip from Alaska to Seattle. Leaving his family, especially his father, had been simple; for there had been no affection in the small-time politician's home in Virginia. Jim is still quite innocent of the women passengers who try to seduce him and of the more worldly cabin boys, one of whom promises to guide him around the more attractive areas of Seattle as soon as the ship arrives there. Young Willard looks forward to proving his manhood with the Seattle prostitutes, although he does not often dream of women: "He missed Bob but not as much as he had a year ago. Except in certain dreams Bob was forgotten" (65).

The two Seattle girls are not undesirable; but Jim, both fascinated and frightened, is repelled by the female's body and runs from the apartment, terrified enough to desert ship but still totally unable to understand his reactions. He is not emotionally sensitive or intellectually acute; in fact, he is able to sleep and forget. Only very slowly does he develop even a slight sympathy for other people and, even more slowly, for himself.

In his nineteenth year, Jim works as a tennis coach for a Beverly Hills hotel, and he is successful because he is athletically talented. During his first really worldly experience, he learns much from the hotel bellboys, who capitalize in every way possible on their physical charms. But Jim is innocently shocked to learn of homosexuality among the boys and among the important film stars and writers of California. Nevertheless, he is pleased to be asked to attend a party at the home of Ronald Shaw, the virile screen idol of countless American women. When Jim almost unemotionally accepts Shaw's invitation to live in his fine home, his education, so long delayed, begins.

Shaw is the first person whom Jim has ever come to know really personally. In spite of his own background—probably more amoral than puritan—Jim comes to enjoy sex with Shaw; and he coolly observes the actor and his homosexual friends. He notices their narcissism, their continuous search for new conquests; but he does not consider himself one of them, for his memory of the weekend with Bob remains a source of self-purification to the unconsciously opportunistic young man. To Jim, Shaw is a revelation in self-pity and "life acting" as he creates emotional crises in order to play the role of the martyr who is never loved so much or so well as he loves.

But, in spite of this fault, Shaw teaches the young man the valuable lesson of acquiring strength: ". . . Shaw had fought and won his battle and he began to teach Jim how to do the same. For such active men as Jim and Ronald Shaw there could be no . . . passive acceptance of the external world's horror; there must be a battle and there must be a victory if they were to survive and be at peace" (102). Jim and Shaw part, basically because of Jim's lack of self-knowledge: "The idea of being in love with a man was still a ludicrous one; still seemed unnatural and rather hopeless: in every case except Bob's and that was different" (110).

Having saved a good deal of money from giving tennis lessons,

Jim takes his freedom and lives with Paul Sullivan, a bitterly disillusioned young writer who has been unsuccessfully married and who appeals to Jim because he is not effeminately homosexual. Their connection is less intense than was Jim's with Shaw, but the young man now "wanted to possess as well as be possessed" (123). When Sullivan mistakenly assumes that Jim is really heterosexual, this assumption may be deliberate, for the writer enjoys pain and mental anguish; he arranges circumstances so that he can savor being betrayed and hurt: "Pain, emotional suffering, finally became an end in itself. . . . He opened himself wide to suffering and he was not disappointed" (135). Jim likes Sullivan's quiet pessimism; and Sullivan, "a lonely man, was less alone with Jim" (136).

However, Jim does not reveal even to Sullivan his inner hope. He "maintained his secret and it grew inside him and became important to him, a part of himself that no one might ever know or share: a memory of a cabin and a brown river. Some day he would relive that again and the circle of his life would be completed. Now he would learn and he would please himself and hide from the outsiders who wanted him to love" (127).

When the two young men spend some time in New Orleans, moving anonymously through the groups of homosexuals, they meet Maria Verlaine, who has long been a friend of Sullivan. Rich, cultured, and lonely, Maria invites the men to visit Yucatán with her. Because she is not herself homosexual, she falls in love with Jim—all at the contrivance of Paul to satisfy his need to suffer. But Jim finds himself unable to consummate the affair with her—his as yet greatest moment of self-awareness. Symbolically, Maria is the Death Goddess who would destroy the young man in her misguided desire for him. Perhaps she does partially destroy the fallacy that Jim has carried along with him: the idea that loving "just one woman" would make him "like other men."

The outbreak of World War II solves the problems of this curious threesome, and Jim and Sullivan enlist. The young man dislikes army life after the freedom of being "one's real self" that he has learned in the circles of homosexuals he has known. Being athletic, Jim becomes a physical training instructor who is left alone by others who think him profound because he is quiet. He rejects the offer of an affair with an older sergeant;

and then, for the first time, he mistakenly approaches the young corporal to whom he is attracted. But no one is very much offended in the relaxed moral atmosphere of wartime. Jim is soon released from the service because of arthritis, from which he has nearly died.

At this point, the current of the novel reverses itself. Until now, Jim has been merely a passive young man, doing little on his own and understanding little that he observes. From Virginia to Seattle to California to New Orleans to Mexico to the army has been quite a modern odyssey. True, Jim has learned a great amount about certain limited areas of life: he has enjoyed a brief, idyllic love in his youth; he has been loved by men who needed him; but he has exerted himself in nothing. However, lying in the army hospital, thinking over his past, Jim begins trying to recapture that past by writing letters to each of the people who had played important parts in that past; he looks back toward the city instead of ahead to the land of future promise.

Vidal describes the effect each of Jim Willard's letters has upon the recipient. Ronald Shaw is not openly very lonely in his chosen role as "the prisoner of fame," but he is more alone than ever; of course, a new boy is living with him. Jim's mother receives his letter as she impatiently waits for death to remove her husband from her unhappy life. Paul Sullivan, agonizing over his wrecked life, hopes to renew his affair with Jim. Maria Verlaine becomes sad at recalling the child she had loved; she now lives only sensually in her search for a perfect man. And Bob Ford, home from the Merchant Marine after five years, hears from Jim on his wedding day: Jim wants to meet Bob again, maybe in New York. Slightly worried, Bob forgets the letter and marries the usual home-town girl from high school days.

After hearing that his father is at last dead, Jim, discharged from the army, goes to New York and works again teaching tennis, finally buying part ownership in a court. At this time he begins the second round of his effort to move backward into his past. He meets Shaw, who takes him to a huge party for homosexuals, given by one of America's richest men, who "supported at least a platoon of soldiers, sailors and marines in New York" (233). He meets Maria, who still searches for the man who can give her perfect love, and Sullivan, who wants to live with Jim again. For the first time, Jim mentions his boyhood lover to someone:

He knew now . . . that he would have to find Bob again before he could be contented and at ease. He was not ready at the moment to search for him but soon, perhaps very soon, he would, and the long journey would end and he and Bob would recapture that mood by the river, the river which had so greatly changed Jim's life and given meaning to his journey. It made him feel strong to think that when he wanted to he could regain the security and completeness he desired, that he could terminate the journey and go home. (254)

When Jim hears from his mother that Bob has married, the information does not especially hurt him; for to him Bob is more worthy of loving if he is "normal." Finally, Jim visits his home, where he is as unhappy and bored as he was in childhood. He meets Bob, having "come back for him"; and they agree to see each other in New York.

When they do meet and go to Bob's room, Bob violently rejects Jim's advances: "Then fury came to Jim, took the place of love"; and, being stronger, Jim strangles his boyhood friend, his imagined perfect lover (306). With Bob dead, Jim goes to drink in a bar "until the dream was completely over" (307). And the novel ends as it began, with Jim drunk and Bob dead; and ". . . it was finished; he was sure of this as he walked in the empty streets. He was changed; if he was not changed he could not live for he had destroyed the most important part of his life, Bob and the legend" (314).

The final effect of *The City and the Pillar* is one of great sympathy and some unfortunate confusion. The protagonist, Jim Willard, is believably presented as a perfectly normal young man, different only in his sexual preference of men rather than women. He is temperamentally in a line with the protagonists of Vidal's previous books—the soldiers of *Williwaw* and the young stockbroker, Robert Holton, of *In a Yellow Wood*. He is never a profound nor an active force, and his understanding is limited to casual observations—insights easily apparent to other people.

The novel succeeds, therefore, in its aim of description; but it breaks down much too often into less than interesting moralizing, making its point through propaganda instead of action. Cocktail parties, bar scenes, intimate conversations—all are occasions for contrived diatribes against the American mother, who competes with men and emasculates her sons, and against a society immature enough to punish what it has created and then has hypocritically treated as undesirable. But perhaps it is too easy to judge this moralizing from a distance of two decades; in 1948, *The City and the Pillar* was a shocking book, and as such it probably deserves credit for helping make the more permissive, less hypocritical social milieu which now regards the book as a sociological as much as a literary phenomenon.

However, *The City and the Pillar* is a moral work. Its subject matter is indeed homosexuality, but the larger theme is concerned with it as only the fringe of the emotional barriers that make love impossible. The great appeal of homosexuality to the reading public since World War II cannot be due simply to morbid interest in a minority of sexual inverts; instead, the difficulties of maintaining homosexual love must reflect a larger, perhaps national inability to achieve the love that is, so it is said, every person's right. Thus Jim Willard's continual denial of significance to new experience demonstrates one larger theme of *The City and the Pillar:* not accepting mutability in human relationships can lead to emotional sterility. Or, as Vidal now considers the point to his novel, ". . . if one continues always to look back, to relate everything to a first affair, one is emotionally, even humanly destroyed. The pillar of salt."[13]

The major flaw of *The City and the Pillar,* one responsible for some confusion, is the ending of the novel—the murder of the beloved by the hysterical lover. It is not at all clear whether this murder is inevitable from the theme or from the story. Is every past not to be relived? Is every dream due to be broken? Does frustration lead, therefore, to violence? Moreover, Jim Willard does not emerge before the end of the novel as a force active enough to avenge in murder the loss of his one support, his insulation from reality. The only defense of this ending—a weak defense indeed—is that the final violence reflects the behavior of the first sexual experience: at the cabin in the woods the sex was initially expressed in playful violence, boyish behavior.

Recognizing this flawed ending and trying to improve the book most closely associated with his name, Vidal has republished it as *The City and the Pillar Revised.* The prose in the new edition is less "raw, youthful, slovenly, true";[14] a great deal of the moralizing is removed; and the ending is made more plausible: Jim forces Bob to submit to a sexual act; then he leaves the room, "prepared to drink until the dream was completely over" (219). Here the depth of Jim's love is believably expressed in the extent of his violent passion. Leaving Bob humiliated and probably wiser, Jim is now free to live in spite of mutability—to look forward again after having looked back and become the pillar of salt.

The revised novel is thematically better written, but one suspects that Vidal rewrote it in order to gain more respect for the novel itself and less notoriety for the legend of the novel as an amazing document from the pen of a very young man. It is impossible not to prefer the philosophy of the revised novel, but it is equally impossible not to like the legend of the 1948 version. Jim Willard, who understands so little about himself and about his world, evidently brought to countless readers invaluable self-understanding.

CHAPTER 3

Misshapen Pearls

A CHARACTER in Gore Vidal's *The Judgment of Paris* is preciously delighted to know that *baroque* in Spanish means "misshapen pearl." With the completion of *The City and the Pillar* late in 1946, Vidal abandoned writing in "the national manner"—one reminiscent of "Hemingway crossed with the gray correctness of *The New Yorker*"[1]—in order to begin the search necessary for every writer: to find his personal style. This quest led him to the awareness that his talent was less adaptable to subdued naturalism than to more baroque ways of writing.

Vidal's search led him into unusual experiments with technique and subject matter. In a quasi-autobiography, a pseudo-medieval prose romance, a nihilistic battle narrative, and diverse short stories, he moved toward the mature style that he perfected just when, for financial reasons, he had to abandon writing novels for a decade.

I The Season of Comfort

Vidal's fourth novel—the novel most young men would have written first—is *The Season of Comfort,* a thinly disguised autobiography.[2] Probably because he was entering a period of experiment when he wanted to concentrate more on technique than on fresh subject matter, he chose to tell in this work the story of his early life. However, *The Season of Comfort* should be read carefully as autobiography; the spirit behind the facts is generally the correct one, but the valuable part of the work is Vidal's feelings about his family and his youth. The novel is an attempt at creating the method a young man uses to look back over his life. What the man is *now* never emerges clearly from the novel, but his origins and the influences acting on him are cleverly revealed.

The Season of Comfort uses seven events in the life of William Giraud, the introspective hero of the novel, to serve as loci from which the past can be seen in flashbacks that reflect several points of view. Scenes from the past alternate with the narration of present action, itself seen from several eyes. The usually brief passages are connected by obvious associations of words or actions parallel in the past and the present. For example, in "The White Flowers," young William Giraud is sent to get flowers from a car for his grandfather's funeral; as he associates this spring and its flowers with a past spring, he thinks of his first two years in school and of the flowery pageant at the end of the second year. The associations are not always handled so obviously, for there are occasionally long passages of uninterrupted, chronological narrative.

"The Beginning," the first section of *The Season of Comfort*, centers around the year 1927 and the birth of William Giraud. The hot Virginia summer is unpleasant for the Hawkins family, especially for Charlotte, who suffers loudly during her first pregnancy. Charlotte has given up an unpromising career in the New York theater to marry Stephen Giraud, son of an old New Orleans family and now a minor government official living unhappily with his wife's family. Charlotte's father is Senator Hawkins, known for his conservatism and for having once been a vice-president. Mrs. Hawkins is a quiet, rather bitter senator's wife.

These four people have among them many curious emotional lines. Charlotte loves her father too insistently and frequently thinks of him as God. Naturally, she hates her mother, who seems forced to compete with the daughter for the senator's affection. Stephen and Charlotte are not happily married, for Charlotte is too ambitious for her husband; she demands from him and from all men the success her father has had. In addition, Charlotte almost unemotionally remembers an incestuous love for her brother, William Hawkins, killed in World War I. Into this interesting family William Giraud is born, painfully for all concerned.

"The Christening" of William Giraud takes place in 1929, when the Giraud family is still living in the Hawkins' home. Only sexual attraction and lack of personal wealth keep Charlotte married to Stephen, who has not advanced satisfactorily in government work. Mrs. Hawkins is devoted to her grandson, although Charlotte has begun to appropriate the boy to herself, loving him too passionately in an attempt to relieve her own dependence frustrations.

This situation parallels Charlotte's past love for her dead brother: "Now there was another William, about to be christened and, in spite of her mother, he was hers, and the William who had been killed had, also though no one knew it, belonged to her, to his sister, the year that he died and she smiled when she thought of this; she had destroyed her mother by taking William from her, she had achieved, in reality, the dream of all daughters" (30).

But William had been killed, and Charlotte was left with one person in whom to believe—her father, who was once literally her God: "She had really believed in God only once and that was when he became presiding officer of the Senate, the Vice-President" (30). And: "The God her mother had taught her to pray to and sing about in the unpleasant dark church at home was, in reality, her own father who sat on a throne" (34).

Stephen Giraud, at his son's christening, remembers having given up painting to marry Charlotte, who now convinces people that she had surrendered a stage career to marry him. Stephen, a man of vague ideas and habits, is never a force equal to his ambitious wife and never a strong father to his son. He likes his mother-in-law; perhaps they unconsciously join forces against Charlotte's scheming, while Senator Hawkins regards them both rather coldly and prefers his grandson to anyone else. "The Christening" of William Giraud ends as "a single drop of water falls on his face" (75).

"The White Flowers," the third section of *The Season of Comfort*, is set in 1940 and is named for the flowers at Senator Hawkins' funeral. In flashbacks, William Giraud remembers his mother's alternating love and hatred for him, the almost regular beatings from her, and her concern that he be socially suave and at the same time very ambitious. Charlotte has divorced Stephen Giraud and married Roger Gilray, a wealthy banker who is gently disillusioned with his ambitious wife but distantly fond of his stepson. Vidal uses this section of his novel to develop sympathy for a young hero victimized by a possessive mother and protected by only a very kind grandfather. But away from his family, Bill does well enough for himself in the boarding schools of Washington, D.C.; and his father tries to help the twelve-year-old boy become aware of the selfishness of his mother, who is tyrannizing over her son by convincing him of his own "selfishness" when he occasionally opposes her. On such occasions, Charlotte justifies all her actions—even her second marriage—by pretending to do everything for her son.

Bill's real escape from his mother is his love for Jimmy Wesson, a friend from boarding school. Publicly, the two boys deplore the sexual experimentation that is endemic to the school's masculine environment; but they both enjoy and learn from their first love affair: ". . . Bill knew vaguely . . . that he and Jimmy were in love; although not even to himself would he use that word. He would far rather die than admit such a thing. But in spite of this, gradually, insidiously, the bodies of women appeared in his dreams and he knew that soon these dreams and their eventual reality would destroy the relationship" (120). The eventual acceptance of heterosexual love will be difficult for Bill because of his mother's warping, sadistic love for him. With his grandfather dead, his grandmother appointed interim senator, and his father a vague man far away, nothing effectually shelters Bill from his mother.

"The King" episode concerns the reception of some obscure European monarch at the Hawkins' home when World War II is imminent. Mrs. Hawkins enjoys being a respected senator; in her power, she has finally triumphed over her daughter's hatred. Stephen Giraud, now an ambassador, comes to the reception, where his ex-wife pointlessly suggests a remarriage. Charlotte has become promiscuous, but she still lacks enough personal fortune to divorce the banker. Bill, at fifteen, has entered a New England academy, where he does not work well enough to satisfy his mother's demands. His father tries again to reveal Charlotte's blind selfishness, but the young man is still confused and unrealistically backward at asserting himself. This reception, bringing together all the principals in Vidal's novel, disappoints them all; for "the King, alas, wore no crown" (166).

"The Winter," centered around Bill's graduation from the unnamed New England academy, covers his three years in the school and his decision, at seventeen, to enlist in the army for World War II. Grandmother Hawkins has died, leaving the family money to Bill when he is twenty-five; his mother is to control his income until then. Stephen Giraud, now important in organizing the United Nations, is to speak at his son's graduation ceremony. He encourages Bill to develop his talent for painting; but Charlotte, who still dominates her son, tells him that painting is unprofitable and that he should do more to please her, "the only person who truly loves him." The three academy years have caused Bill and Jimmy to travel different paths—Bill, to art and artistic friends; Jimmy, to athletics and the popular boys. But, in his painting and in his new friendships, Bill Giraud has not emerged as a young man sure of himself and his goals: his responses are automatic; he feels nothing very deeply, even his debilitating dependence on his shrewish mother.

Too predictably, Vidal introduces his young protagonist to heterosexual experience—an unsatisfying group action with a girl from the academy town. However, this episode leads to a more serious flaw in the novel—an old-fashioned girl-understands-boy scene. The girl, an art student at a nearby women's school, encourages Bill to do what he really wishes to do, promising him that, no matter what he may lose, *she* will be there. But Vidal fortunately does not ask the reader to accept a total about-face in his hero's attitude toward women: ". . . he did not fall in love. He wondered if he ever could. He liked her, however, more than anyone else he could think of, his family, naturally, excepted. She also appealed to him physically but most important of all they understood the same things; their awareness of the world was the same. Yet he couldn't love her" (209).

The emphasis on winter as despair, on spring as hope, and on summer as the promise of freedom for Bill Giraud is maintained throughout this section of *The Season of Comfort,* preparatory to "The Parallel Construction," in which Bill and his mother have their final quarrel and separate. Vidal uses a strange printing device to make this scene brief, sufficiently bitter, and revelatory enough to convince the reader that this is a final separation of mother and son. On recto and verso pages, respectively, the spoken and unspoken words of mother and son are juxtaposed. All the accusations of selfishness spoken by the mother and all her past lies, distortions, and true selfishness remembered by the son lead to Bill's final words: "'As far as I'm concerned you can go to hell and I'm leaving now since that's what you want. I sometimes think I've always hated you.' Now he would leave.

He was shaking. The pain, the pain; it hurt but he would leave' "
(242). At the same time, Charlotte says and thinks: "He's leaving. . . . 'I've always hated you.' He's always hated me? Oh my
God, what's happened? He's leaving. He has always hated me"
(243).

The final section of *The Season of Comfort* repeats the title
of the first part, "The Beginning." It is May, 1945; and Bill has
recuperated in France from a battle wound. He no longer remembers exactly why he entered the army, nor is he especially
concerned with experiencing battle or adventure or with antici-
pating civilian life. On this particular day, he receives letters
which both confirm and confuse him. His father writes sympa-
thetically of Bill's mother, but the young man resists the temp-
tation of reconciliation with her.

Two letters from the artistic fiancée speak quietly of her faith
in him: "As much as he doubted love this must be it. Perhaps
it might yet be possible to have love without violence. Now love
was offered him and it appeared large and constant. And he
didn't know if he could believe or answer" (251). A letter from
a school friend tells of the death of Bill's adolescent lover, Jimmy
Wesson. Vidal's hero is now rather like an ancient, ruined arch
near the army hospital in France: the arch itself is unbroken,
the frame for the door is intact, but no one now cares where the
door led. He has discovered that there is no season of comfort,
that "spring, like the other seasons, was bitter" (253).

The Season of Comfort is thus a young man's book, written
in resentment as retribution for real or imagined wrongs. As with
all "grudge-writing," this novel appeals most strongly to readers
who share the author's bitterness—in this case, hatred for having
been defiled by a passionate, domineering mother. However,
when considered as autobiography, *The Season of Comfort* seems
scrupulously careful to explain and illustrate why the Giraud
family and the Hawkins family behave as they do. And none
of the relationships revealed—Oedipal love, incest, homosexuality
—is anything other than a basic emotional pattern in exaggerated
extension. The ills of these characters are legion, but no act could
have prevented them or their consequences. The rebellion of
William Giraud is predictable from his sharing in the universal
nature of being a young man; the sadness is that he must refight
the old battles in each new relationship.

The Season of Comfort is a true but flawed novel. Vidal works so hard at determining what constituted his childhood that the young man supposedly making these examinations is almost non-existent. The grandfather and grandmother, the mother and father, the boyhood friend and the adolescent fiancée—all these people exist, most of them vividly; but William Giraud is only a colorless force re-creating them. Vidal says that the hero is devoted to his mother, that he is strong among his friends, that he paints well; but the reader never feels that Giraud is really doing anything or that he could ever be doing anything but re-creating his past. For Giraud to realize, after his sad experiences, that there is no season of comfort is admirable; but for him now to be nothing and to show promise of nothing negates the validity of the search into his physical and emotional origins.

The Season of Comfort is important in Vidal's work as an experiment and as a failure. The technique of using flashbacks connected by symbols that are parallel in the past and in the present is reminiscent of a movie not well edited: the pieces can fit together well enough to tell a story only if the viewer sees the film several times. The "parallel construction" could have become a promising literary (instead of printing) device if human eyes could read two pages simultaneously. And, finally, the protagonist could have been a powerful creation if he had been more than an empty stand-in for the author. Fortunately for Gore Vidal, the author gave promise of more achievement than did his fictional self.

II A Search for the King

"From the time I was five and could read," recalls Gore Vidal, "until I was ten or eleven . . . I read everything I could and ruined my eyes and cluttered my memory with all sorts of ghosts whom I can no longer identify, characters and events which haunt me still with their insistent anonymity. But one story I've remembered clearly. I believe it was in the set called *The Book of Knowledge* and I reread it often, pondered it and, finally, in the fall of 1947 I decided to make a book of it."[3]

The work which resulted is *A Search for the King*, Vidal's fifth novel and his first departure from using modern settings. The subject of *A Search for the King* is the quest for Richard I by Blondel de Néel, his troubadour and companion. Richard, known as Coeur de Léon or Lion-Hearted and the third son of Henry II, became king of England in 1189 and immediately prepared to conduct the third crusade. After the crusade, according to history, Richard was captured by Leopold of Austria and held by Emperor Henry VI. According to legend, however, at least that in the thirteenth-century *Chronicle of Rheims,* Richard was sought by his troubadour, Blondel, who sang beneath Richard's window and then reported the king's imprisonment to England. Ransomed by the English nation, Richard returned to England and fought his usurping brother John in March, 1195. In *A Search for the King,* Vidal wisely ignores history and reconstructs Blondel's quest in order to demonstrate the idea of friendship and betrayal.[4]

A Search for the King covers the time from the autumn of 1192 to March 28, 1194. Entitled "The Capture," the first part of the novel tells of Blondel's observation of the port of Zara on the Adriatic, where Richard and his men have landed to begin riding across Europe toward England. The crusades have already made different peoples more aware of and tolerant of one another: "It was better now . . . than in the days before the first Crusade when strangers were apt to be stoned to death as a matter of policy. The armies, however, had changed all that. People were now quite used to companies of men moving from west to east and, later, returning, scarred and seldom richer, from east to west" (14).

Richard, disguised as a monk and angry as he so often is, hopes to cross Austria safely. Richard "was graying and deep lines curved to the corners of his small mouth, half hidden by a short beard. He was a handsome man and vain; yet, though vain, he disliked ugly faces and he always had handsome people around him" (15). Blondel, Richard's favorite troubadour, and two other companions are to accompany the king across Europe while most of the men travel as another company.

Composing ballads as they ride, the king's company travels across Austria: "The fields stretched for miles before them; fields separated by woods and centered about villages and occasional castles. This time of year the fields were dark, stubbled, the color of the earth, and the sun shone, when it shone, bright and hard.

The air was clear and the wind blew sharply, cooled the days, created a singular clarity, knocked red leaves from the trees" (20).

Richard worries about affairs in England. Having begun the crusade shortly after being crowned, the king is not well known in his own country. His brother John is rumored to be usurping the kingly powers; this rumor is partially responsible for Richard's decision to return to England. A more immediate worry is vengeance from Austrian relatives of the Marquis of Montferrat, murdered during a quarrel over spoils after Richard's victory over the Saracens at Acre. Blondel suspects Richard as the murderer, but Richard claims innocence although he admits his happiness about Montferrat's death. Richard is not especially acute, Blondel thinks: ". . . he almost never looked people directly in the face because his close-set eyes made them nervous: cold and watchful eyes that appeared to see so much and actually, Blondel knew, saw very little, did not care to recognize another's reality or another's dream" (25-26).

At Goritz, the king tries to sell a family jewel for food; but the Lord of Goritz recognizes the ornament and orders the company out of town. Continuing westward into a forest, rumored to be haunted, the men successfully fight a fierce dragon, which is as real in *A Search for the King* as in any medieval romance; and the reaction of the men is more believable: they fight it as they would any other beast of prey, never doubting that there are indeed dragons in plenitude.

Another of Montferrat's relatives tries to capture Richard; but he, Blondel, and young William escape and find new provisions at the castle of their would-be captors. Again they travel, and again Blondel envies men of towns and castles—people who believe "that Kings felt no discomfort if they were brave, that Saracens were evil and Christians good, that the crusades were begun to free the tomb of Christ" (49). To Richard's credit, he admits—at least privately—that the crusades are instigated by considerations of "loot, trade routes and strategic positions" and by the desire to provide young knights with battlegrounds outside England.

Blondel considers fighting "poignant, of course, yet beautiful, containing as all great beauty must, the tragic proportion" (51). The troubadour compares battle to his ballads, which are sad, even though they deal with love. Courtly love to Blondel is more than love of an ideal lady: "For the Lady was many things: all love, all great emotions, battles. The Lady was the comradeship of knights. The Lady was beauty. The Lady was the mother of God. So she stood as a symbol for many things, for all the passion and all the beauty in the world" (51). Throughout *A Search for the King*, Vidal speaks through Blondel, who quietly wonders about battle, romance, friendship, and his own devotion to Richard—the ultimate point of the novel.

But first the device of the search is set up when Richard is taken into "friendly captivity" by Leopold, Duke of Vienna. Richard commissions Blondel to report his capture to England, knowing that the Queen Mother Eleanor will arrange his release. When the troubadour begins traveling westward, he never uses his real name for fear of capture. When he finds an English knight and sends him to Eleanor with news of Richard's captivity, Blondel is free to search for his lord.

Hearing that Richard is being held at Tiernstein, Blondel travels in that direction through a dark forest, where he is entertained by werewolves—men who live in a forest lair and survive by robbing travelers. Of Blondel the thieves want only his music. At the castle of Tiernstein, Blondel learns that Richard has been there but is now elsewhere. He is welcomed by the guard captain, whose "face was sad, the face of one of the Nordic gods, beautiful yet curiously weak: a god whose strength had been dissipated when his people turned to Christianity, no longer putting flowers on his altar" (88-89).

The lord and lady of the castle are delighted with the new minstrel; the lady forces Blondel to spend the night entertaining her, threatening to accuse him of attacking her unless he obliges. Blondel "wondered often in the course of that dreadful night if any King had ever been so well served as Richard was by him" (97). As he again wanders along, Blondel thinks of Richard's interest in war and money, of the king's ballads, of his own lovemaking—he is "a being, momentarily divorced from time, separate from the world: he existed now and that was enough; he moved, a single star from darkness to darkness falling" (101).

When Blondel next visits a peasant family, he helps the men work; and he seduces the young niece, whom he finds admirably practical in wishing once to love a handsome stranger: "It should happen once like this, I think. Now I can marry one of the village boys and have children and be like all the other women here except that I'll be able to think about this" (105). This memory made, the troubadour leaves the girl, aware that it is

> better to meet someone for an instant, to hold another body close to one's own, to be, for an instant, a single creature, part of another with a similar will and then to part, to desert this magic for ordinary living and a search for the King, equipped thus with only pleasant memory, separating before boredom has destroyed the magic in one's arms, before the sad awakening that one has touched another person, a separate being and unknown. So much better to go from lover to lover, from instant to instant, performing the ritual of completion and then, with new memory, go walking again in the clear air of a winter day, remembering only the enchantment, the complemented rhythm of another's body, existing at last as personal fantasy, unshared and, finally, possessed: a memory of fire and constant as fire is not. (108-9)

Next Blondel encounters a giant, who, as a fellow craftsman, invites the troubadour home to listen to Latin pastorals and to share dinner. A choir boy until he had obtained his growth, the giant has only one fault outside his poetry: he enjoys the shepherd boys from among the hills. Blondel, being safely beyond boyhood, is merely amused over a giant's being a sexual creature until dinner is served: the boy is cooked satisfactorily tender. After this humorous adventure, Vidal guides his hero back to his serious quest; for Blondel yearns

> to be in one place with one person . . . [for] now he was lost, without a center, quite alone, and he was terrified. . . . For an instant he saw the entire world: menacing and, worst of all, impersonal in its cruelty. He was part of continual change: he would age and his body would become weak and his face loose, grotesque. His voice would go and then what would he do? where would he go to live the last years of his life, the years of ugliness? If anything happened to Richard he would be lost, without protection. . . ." (121-22)

Frequently Vidal seems to be remembering in *A Search for the King* those poems in Old English that tell of the thane's longing for his lord—"Wanderer," "Seafarer," and "Widsith."

In Vienna, the troubadour wins a handsome prize when he sings before the imperial court and Duke Leopold; however, Richard is at Lintz while the duke and the emperor quarrel over sharing the eventual ransom money. Leaving Vienna, Blondel continues onward, knowing that "only a few . . . realize, if only vaguely, that they must find a king; although the search itself is enough reason to forget one's history, sufficient cause to destroy the fact of the future which is at best, an abstraction and a dream" (138).

But the emperor has seized Richard and taken him away; so the troubadour again wanders on his journey, visiting a dull country castle and escaping from the Countess Valeria, vampire and philosopher of death. After traveling with a priest who disputes over faith, reason, love, good, and evil, Blondel is at last near his king, who is to be tried by the emperor for the murder at Acre and for having compromised with the Saracens.

In "The Return," covering the events of spring of 1193, Vidal quickens his narrative; for the search itself ends when Blondel sings in public to Richard of a captive "heart" and Richard in response sings the story of his own betrayal by the English nobility. Blondel must now return to England to start arrangements for Richard's release. Before reaching Paris, the troubadour accepts as constant companion a blond German youth named Karl, who accompanies him to England. England has assumed Richard to be dead; and the king's brother John, who has allied himself with Phillip of France, claims the loyalty of much of the English nation. When Blondel reports that Richard is alive and angry for not having been released, Queen Eleanor promises to arrange the excommunication of Richard's captors; and John is upset at the news of his brother's being alive.

"The Battle," the final section of *A Search for the King*, takes place on March 29, 1194. The armies of John and Richard fight near Nottingham, after Richard's ransom in Germany and his gathering an army in France. Blondel and the boy Karl take part in this battle, where survival comes by skill and chance and where, aided by the men loyal to Robin Hood, Richard wins the right again to wear his crown. Medieval blood spills over the English meadows much as American blood spills at Chancellorsville in Crane's *The Red Badge of Courage* (1895); there is no more honor or glory among the men dying in mail than among the men dying later in modern war machines. The battle is the same confusion, seen by Blondel, by Karl, and by Richard.

But Karl is one of the dead, killed in his first battle: "Blondel put his head in his lap. A cold rain fell, an early spring rain, but he was not aware of it. He remained a long time. It had ended; his own youth lay dead in the rain and he'd be old now, unprotected, centered in himself and never young again. The wind, shrill-sounding, full of rain, raked the meadow, blew through Sherwood Forest. The twilight, thick with rain clouds, was almost as dark as night" (255).

A Search for the King, although written in Vidal's second or experimental period, does not employ the technical devices used in *The Season of Comfort*—the shifting point of view; the brief, impressionistic flashbacks; the parallel construction. In fact, the work is closer to Vidal's first novel, *Williwaw*, than to any other of his works: it is a simple story, told with an economy of language and sentiment. But in its rather florid imagery and its curious mixture of dream and reality, *A Search for the King* resembles the mood poems of John Keats more than the narratives of Lord Byron, probably because Keats himself was more deeply influenced by the medieval romances.

Vidal manages to retell the medieval story of Blondel's search without offending the modern reader's conception of a medieval tale. The hero is spotlessly bright, if he is Blondel. If Richard is considered the hero of *A Search for the King*, then he is more human in this novel than in any medieval tale: he is greedy, vicious, opportunistic, hypocritical in public, but very brave in adversity and always tender toward Blondel. The landscape itself in this almost picaresque story is as important as the characters. Changing in time with Blondel's moods and with the seasons, the landscape is ideally stylized while the facts of daily medieval life are realistically pictured. The dirt, poverty, provincialism, and ugliness are contrasted with the beauty of nature.

But *A Search for the King* is more than a pseudo-medieval tale of adventure or a romantic poem of atmosphere. In Blondel's search for Richard can be seen a reflection of the eternal need of all men to have "centers" for their lives—values worthy of their devotion. The presence of such a center should never be made prerequisite to every work of fiction, but it can be studied in the life of any one character. And surely Blondel's quest for

Richard is Vidal's examination of the fact of loneliness and his attempt to demonstrate the need for a center. The best illustration of this relationship between the troubadour and his king is Carson McCullers' philosophy of love, presented first in her *Ballad of the Sad Café* (1943):

> There are the lover and the beloved, but these two come from different countries. Often the beloved is only a stimulus for all the stored-up love which has lain quiet within the lover for a long time. And somehow every lover knows this. He feels in his soul that his love is a solitary thing . . . the lover about whom we are speaking need not necessarily be a young man saving for a wedding-ring—this lover can be man, woman, child, or indeed any human creature on this earth. Now the beloved can also be of any description. The most outlandish people can be the stimulus for love. . . . The preacher may love a fallen woman. The beloved may be treacherous, greasy-headed and given to evil habits. Yes, and the lover may see this as clearly as anyone else —but that does not affect the evolution of his love one whit. . . . The value and quality of any love is determined solely by the lover himself.[5]

This conception of love, applied to *A Search for the King*, justifies the disconcerting fact that Richard is not worthy of Blondel's devotion but that, to Blondel, Richard is *the* satisfactory center for his life and thus worthy beyond question. But after the battle, when Blondel sees Karl dead and realizes that "his own youth" is dead, he may be wondering, along with the reader, whether serving Richard has been ultimately the best possible way of life: Richard fought and killed a dragon, but Karl rode a unicorn.

III Dark Green, Bright Red

For *Dark Green, Bright Red*,[6] Vidal chose an exotic, modern setting. His sixth novel, and the third and last in his period of experimentation, *Dark Green, Bright Red* is set in a present-day "banana republic" of Central America. Vidal obviously drew his knowledge of Central America from having lived in Guatemala, where he finished writing *Dark Green, Bright Red* in early 1949. Although the least interesting of his ten novels, it stands in style just at the doorway of the two "Edgewater" novels—*The Judgment of Paris* and *Messiah*—in which he finally demonstrated mastery of all the components of long fiction.

Dark Green, Bright Red is the story of a revolutionary movement in "the Republic," one never specifically named. The protagonist is Peter Nelson, a mysterious young man from the United States and a West Point graduate who has recently been court-martialed. The reader never learns the offense behind the military discipline nor, indeed, very much at all about Nelson, who is in the Republic as a mercenary soldier hired to train natives into an army for General Jorge Alvarez Asturias.

General Asturias has returned to the Republic after spending many years in comfortable exile in New Orleans; his nineteen-year tyranny over his country was overthrown by Señor Ospina, a former professor of mathematics and leader of the nation's young people, eager for a revolution to wrest power from their domineering elders. Asturias has accepted Ospina's invitation to return to his home, ostensibly to run and lose in the first free election in decades—an election held only to impress the United States Department of State that is at least publicly wary of Latin American dictators.

The General is "neither tall nor short, neither fat nor thin: he existed as a personality, a voice, a face, a head. Like many rulers he tended to be more general than particular: the reflection of many people's opinion of him. His personality was enigmatic, his manner rational. He invariably became whatever the person or group with him expected him to be; yet always he stood a bit beyond, separate; and he encompassed and directed them just as they seemed to encompass and direct him" (19-20). But General Asturias has selected men to help him run his revolution, men who will share the advantages of his again being dictator. The leaders are to move into the North of the Republic, where the General's public support should be strongest and where "the fruit Company," the real power of the Republic, can secretly back the movement.

First of these leaders is José Alvarez, son of the General, who has returned with his father from exile in the United States. José is his father's delight and probably his successor to the presidency, should the General die in office after the revolution. In the United States, José was the rich playboy; in the United

States Army, he was the all-around "good fellow" and, inciden-
tally, the best friend of Peter Nelson, who has come to the Republic at José's invitation.

Charles de Cluny, second among the conspirators, has been
the General's speech-writer and secretary for ten years. Author
of many second-rate novels in France in the 1930's, de Cluny
drifted into the General's service because he feared repeating
his "best writing." De Cluny delights in shocking Father Miguel,
the Catholic priest necessary to the conspiracy and anxious to
become archbishop under the General's restored rule. Colonel
Aranhas, a native Indian, is the military leader of the revolution,
which is to seem to be a popular uprising of the oppressed
Indians.

Asturias holds his first staff meeting at his home in Tenango,
the second city of the Republic: "Tenango and, in fact, most of
the country was situated on a plateau a mile above the two great
oceans which broke upon the bejungled and malarial beaches
of the Republic, strips of hot banana country framing, on two
sides, the plateau where most of the people lived and worked,
producing coffee and sticky-eyed children, thus insuring the future production of both, presumably forever" (12).

There are, of course, two more conspirators to round out the
cast—Elena Alvarez, the General's daughter, who is too much
beloved by her brother; and Colonel Rojas, who is to take the
capital for the revolution. These stock characters go through all
the usual movements preparatory to the battles: José and Peter
Nelson train a few hundred natives who are more interested in
killing personal enemies and in looting towns than in liberating
their country; Mr. Green of the fruit company appears with his
son to promise arms and further the courtship of the son and
Elena; and Peter Nelson patiently waits for Elena to succumb
to his physical charms.

Nelson is always afraid that someone besides José will learn
of his court-martial; but, whatever his crime was, he never worries over his guilt. Having no apparent goals of his own, he cares
nothing for those of the revolution. He easily sees through the
public motives of the conspirators: the General, growing old,
wants absolute power once again; the company wants to perpetu-
ate its holdings and satisfy its American owners; the priest wants

to rule the national church; Colonel Aranhas wants military power; de Cluny enjoys playing the faithful secretary; and José, a brainless dolt, enjoys training men to fight.

But Nelson is capable of being lonely in a strange country. Although he claims to be eager for only "some money and loving and only a small measure of prestige," he is a modern-day gentleman of fortune: "We're all adventurers now. Nobody stays where he was born any more; nobody does the same job till he dies. We all move around from city to city, from town to town, from one group to another. We're all traveling: that's the condition of our time and we seem, in spite of reactionaries who'd like us dancing on the village green, to thrive on this sort of life, to live longer, to do more things" (81-82).

The intrigues of the conspiracy multiply as the day of march nears. The General's army is to move southward to take the cities of Nadatenango and Tenango—victories that are to cause the government to capitulate. Before the day of action arrives, traitors are discovered, tortured, and shot; the native soldiers prove to be of good marksmanship, if of dubious courage; and Peter Nelson still anticipates his affair with Elena. "Dark Green" ends as the company marches southward, through the jungle, to its first revolutionary battle.

"Bright Red" reveals the army on the plain near Nadatenango. The city is taken only after considerable fighting, for the General's soldiers were braver than anyone had expected. After the excitement of battle, before the army marches to Tenango, Peter Nelson and Elena begin their more sensual than secret affair, in spite of Nelson's cynical attitude toward love:

Only once had he loved anyone and he had been wretched. Once was enough. He had no wish to repeat that experience and it was, he thought, unlikely that he ever would. He would satisfy the body and he would try to satisfy a vague need for companionship. He would be less solitary if possible but he knew how useless it was to expect ever to possess completely or to be possessed: the beast with the two backs had, after all, two brains and two identities and it was neither possible nor desirable to fuse them, to lose identity. The act made a momentary union, an instant of sharing, of identification, but this passed in a single second to be recalled later as pleasure and little more. (103)

Their affair of doubtful joy is the last act of the conspirators to go as planned or hoped. José, knowing of his sister's attraction to his best friend, kills himself by wrecking his jeep. The General, dispirited by his son's suicide, displays only perfunctory leadership over his troops who desperately want to desert and must be guarded by their officers. With success no longer assured, the conspirators and their army march into Tenango, which surrenders bloodlessly to the General; it is strange that the garrison has been removed to the capital by Colonel Rojas. The northern army begins to drink or desert, having mysteriously learned that all is not going smoothly for the revolution. Colonel Aranhas refuses to pay the soldiers for their work of revolution —a confusing action until it is revealed that he is in reality an agent for the government in power. That government has been taken over by Colonel Rojas, backed by the company. Obviously, the whole revolution was planned by Rojas in order to appear a popular hero by seizing—"temporarily," of course—the presidency of the Republic.

The revolution over and all ambitions of the General's conspirators frustrated, Peter Nelson quickly leaves the Republic, having carefully assured himself a route of escape. He wonders:

> Where shall I go and what must I do? The familiar questions remained, as usual, unanswered. It was enough to know that, for the moment, he was in danger, in flight. He had always, it had seemed, been in flight, in danger, even though, of course, within the various designs there had been no true repetitions. The recent comedy had, more than once, engrossed him so much that he had forgotten, from time to time, that all of the speeches had been delivered to an empty house while, at best, only a personal sense of virtue had been served by any action. Nothing was real for nothing had touched him. (306)

In the word "comedy" rests whatever merit Vidal's novel may have. Read seriously, the plot of armed revolution seems hopelessly worn, probably because just such revolutions occur so frequently in Latin America that a fictional one is third-hand material. The involvement of mercenaries, church officials, and American investors is quite commonplace knowledge, as are the official posturings these men assume: Democrats, Republicans, or Socialists—all the principals act purely selfishly. *Dark Green, Bright Red* can be considered, therefore, only a tame exposé.

And the protagonist, Peter Nelson, emerges as the least interesting hero in Vidal's fiction. Less like a militant Robert Holton than a mercenary Richard II, Nelson's background, thoughts, and actions are so very dull that one wonders whether Vidal meant him to be taken seriously. True, Nelson can tell himself as he flees the Republic that his experiences there did have meaning:

> Yet he had cared for Elena and for José, and the fighting had terrified him. He frowned in the sunlight, aware that although the design was illusory and not constant it was often, in spite of its artifice, engaging and, too, as each minute passed, he moved into yet another, and so far unrevealed, design in which, again bemused, he would act and he would, often for long moments indeed, know an ease and a spontaneous loving which would make him forget what he knew: that there was no audience and no response, only the need to speak and, finally, finally, to pretend. (306)

But no pretensions of Peter Nelson could be superior as fiction to those stories of male adventures to be found in cheap sportsmen's magazines.

Although *Dark Green, Bright Red* fails in story and characters, the novel may be considered successful in theme if read as a satire on revolutionary movements. In the mixture of public and private motives and native and foreign conspirators, the work resembles, except in its bloodshed and lust, the idea operating in the comic operas of Gilbert and Sullivan: nothing is what it seems. The office of president conceals a dictatorship; the populace never deserves or gets democracy; and the whole revolution, engineered by non-revolutionaries, is led by a general (power of the right claiming to be the left) against the president (in the center but claiming to be the left), while the intellectuals (leftists who in office become corrupt themselves) never are important.

It is in prose style, however, that *Dark Green, Bright Red* assumes an important place in the canon of Vidal's fiction. The individual sentences and paragraphs frequently reveal the sharp wit that makes the "Edgewater" novels and the later plays successful. Vidal writes of the citizens of the Republic: "Before the

Spanish they had had no music, no art, no literature: they still have no music, no art, no literature and here, thought Peter, sitting down on the edge of the patio, I am" (12). The General censored newspapers because "they print libel, given half a chance. They don't understand what it is to tell the truth, to represent what they dislike as it is rather than as they would like it to be" (55). The battles must be fought soon because ". . . there was just so much money and the timetable for the revolution operated according to the amount of money they had. Well, it would be a short campaign; *that* was a good thing" (129). This tone of light irony, not the imitative interior monologues or the incomplete symbolism (Mr. Green—Bright Green? Rojas—Red?), marks in *Dark Green, Bright Red* Vidal's progress toward finding his most successful writing style.

IV A Thirsty Evil

The relative unpopularity and financial failure of *The Season of Comfort, A Search for the King,* and *Dark Green, Bright Red* —published after *The City and the Pillar*—caused Vidal to abandon fiction for drama in the mid-1950's. However, he soon interrupted work on drama to publish a small collection of his short stories, *A Thirsty Evil.*[7] These seven stories, written between 1948 and 1956, reveal a considerable talent for short fiction, a talent Vidal has not cultivated more extensively because the short story does not sell easily and because his subject matter is often not to the taste of most potential buyers. The stories in *A Thirsty Evil,* of clearly unequal merit, deal with three subjects—childhood, "appearance and reality," and homosexuality.

"The Robin," written in 1948 and apparently autobiographical, tells of an experience in the narrator's childhood, when he "enjoyed all sorts of unpleasant things: other people's fights . . . automobile accidents, stories of suicides and one particular peepshow at an amusement park near Washington where, through holes in a tall imitation stockade, one could observe an immense plaster elephant goring a plaster Hindu" (33). The child dreamed of being strong enough to torture his enemies, especially his fourth-grade teacher, "a shapeless woman with bobbed hair, gray and untidy. . . . She was stern, malicious and, in moments of anger, an arm-twister. She received her reward in *my* world" (35).

Preferring outdoor play to indoor classroom boredom, the boy and his friend Oliver, one day playing apart from their classmates, find an injured robin, unable to fly, and decide to kill it mercifully. They stone the bird until its cries of pain force them to crush its head: "We stood for a long time, not looking at one another, the pile of stones between us. No sound but the distant shouts of our classmates playing on the lawn. The sun shone brilliantly; nothing had changed in the world but suddenly, without a word and at the same moment, we both began to cry" (40-41).

In the second story of childhood, "A Moment of Green Laurel" (1949), the narrator is a young man who, after living through World War II, has returned to Washington to witness the inauguration of a President. He wanders into the Willard Hotel and then into an inaugural party upstairs where he meets his mother. They have little to discuss, although they have been separated for some years. Later, in a mood of reminiscence, the young man walks beyond the city toward his childhood home. Outside the stately country house, he meets a small boy who is gathering laurel to weave into Roman wreaths that the narrator had also made in his childhood at the house. The boy lives with his grandfather, reads in the attic of the house, and is called for supper by a name familiar to the narrator, who wonders "as I walked away, down the road between the dark evening hills . . . if I should ever recall an old encounter with a stranger who had asked me odd questions about our house, and about the green laurel which I carried in my arms" (55).

"The Ladies in the Library," written in 1950, is Vidal's first story to use the convention of appearance versus reality. A modern version of the Greek fable of the Parcae—the three fates who spin, weave, and end man's life—the story tells of the visit of a middle-aged writer and his older cousin to the old family home in Virginia. Walter and Sybil, the last members of the Bragnet family, are unmarried; for Walter, at fifty-one, cares for only his writing, and Sybil is interested in only her numerous dogs and cats. These two visit Miss Mortimer, now mistress of the Bragnet mansion, who invites the "Parker" sisters to a reception. Walter inadvertently hears the three sisters planning his death over their knitting. As they agree that he is to die from a heart attack, one sister cuts the knot in her yarn; and Walter "could neither speak nor move now. He was conscious of a massive constriction in his chest. As he gasped for breath, nearly blind in the sun, Miss Mortimer appeared to him over the edge of the receding world, and he saw that she was smiling, a summer flower in her gleaming hair, a familiar darkness in her lovely eyes" (154). A deceptive normality conceals in this story an even more fanciful nemesis.

"Erlinda and Mr. Coffin," written in 1951, also deals with appearance and reality but represents one of Vidal's few early attempts at humor. Mrs. Craig, the narrator and "a gentlewoman in middle life," is a descendant of a fine Carolina family much reduced in wealth and a widow since the Depression of 1929: "In olden times my social activities in this island city were multifarious, but since 1929 I have drawn in my horns, as it were, surrendering all my high offices in the various organizations with which our city abounds to one Marina Henderson, wife of our local shrimp magnate and a cultural force to be reckoned with in these parts not only because her means are ample but because our celebrated Theater-in-the-Egg is the child of her teeming imagination: she is Managing Directress, Star and sometime Authoress" (23). Mrs. Craig supplements her small legacy by "giving shelter to paying guests."

This gentlewoman's dignity and income end, unfortunately, when she rents shelter in her home to a Mr. Coffin and his ward, a small colored girl, eight years old, named Erlinda Lopez. The charming girl is so gracious that Marina Henderson offers her the leading role in her own blank-verse adaptation of *Camille*. This part seems surprisingly natural to the child until, Marina's advances rejected by Erlinda, Marina assumes the title role herself. At the first performance, however, Erlinda has her revenge; for Marina calls for more tapers, more light:

Then it happened. Erlinda picked up the candelabra and held it aloft for a moment, a superhuman effort since it was larger than she; then, taking aim, she hurled it at Marina who was instantly ignited. Pandemonium broke loose in the theater! Marina, a pillar of fire, streaked down the aisle and into the night: she was subdued at last in the street by two policemen who managed to put out the blaze, after which they removed her to the hospital where she now resides, undergoing at this moment her twenty-fourth skin graft. (101)

GORE VIDAL

Arrested for assault and battery, Erlinda is discovered to be, of course, a forty-one-year-old dwarf and the bride of Mr. Coffin.

These four stories of childhood and illusion are cleverly written, especially "Erlinda and Mr. Coffin"; but they are of really slight worth in comparison with the three remaining stories in *A Thirsty Evil*, which deal with homosexuality. The first, "Three Stratagems," was written in 1950, two years after the publication of *The City and the Pillar*. The first part of this story is narrated by Michael, a young male prostitute or "hustler" who caters in Key West to rich vacationers who play his game—a sinister one if, being wise, "they enjoy their own degradation." When Michael meets Mr. Royal, he carefully evaluates his chances with the widower from New England; and Mr. Royal invites Michael to dine that night in his hotel room.

The second part of "Three Stratagems" is narrated by Mr. Royal, who sees in Michael the first possible fulfillment of his dream of having the love and companionship of youth. He realizes that "it's no worse to be loved for one's money than to be loved for something as spurious and impermanent as beauty. One must be practical and the thing to bear in mind, I've found, is not *why* one receives certain attentions but the attentions themselves" (23).

The intimate dinner goes well, and the evening promises fulfillment; but suddenly Michael suffers a seizure of epilepsy. Mr. Royal's commentary ends the story:

So, for the time at least, the ghost is vanished, obscured and distorted by that figure among the shattered dishes upon the floor. I haven't talked to him since although I did see him earlier today on the beach. We did not speak. He was with an old friend of mine, a man named Jim Howard. Jim is a grand fellow about my age or, perhaps, a little older. At one time he was very wealthy but he hasn't a dime now. They seem to be getting on very well, however, and it will be interesting to see what happens. (30-31)

"The Zenner Trophy," also written in 1950, is, in spite of its youthful idealism, one of the few really good American stories about homosexuality. Set at a New England preparatory school, this story is told from the point of view of Mr. Beckman, a quietly professional, rather elderly teacher who is given the unpleasant task of informing Flynn, one of his advisees, of the student's expulsion a week before his graduation. The school is embarrassed over having to expel its top athlete because he has been caught with his friend, another outstanding athlete, in "an intimate situation." Because the academy has already announced that Flynn has been awarded the Carl F. Zenner Trophy for Clean Sportsmanship, his expulsion will doubtless further embarrass that proper institution.

Mr. Beckman sadly accepts his duty and finds Flynn calmly packing to leave, his companion already having left the campus. He is amazed that Flynn shows no regret or shame, only anger at learning that his parents have needlessly, in his view, been told of the affair. Flynn explains his optimism: his athletic prowess will guarantee him acceptance and money at any university; and his friend and he are going to attend their state university together. Their lives are happy; only Mr. Beckman's life is sad now. He reluctantly admires two young men who dare to live as though their private lives were completely their own concern. Because he has never known what he has never dared, the old man is now "aware there was nothing left that he could do" (80).

A cynical, more mature story is "Pages from an Abandoned Journal," written especially for publication in *A Thirsty Evil*. As the title suggests, this story is in the form of lengthy diary entries, supposedly selected from a journal kept by an American graduate student living in Europe while writing his dissertation for a doctorate in history from Columbia University. Written from 1948 to 1953, these entries reveal the effect of European life on an American "innocent," but one ready to be educated by the older society.

For April 30, 1948, the young man recounts his violent protests made the previous night to homosexual advances in a Paris bar. He reminds himself to write Helen, the fiancée in America; then he visits (socially) an aging male prostitute, the renowned lover of the great and the near-great. The learning of the homosexuals affronts the American: "I sat and talked for a while with an interior decorator from New York and, as usual, I was floored by the amount these people know: painting, music, literature, architecture . . . where do they learn it all? I sit like a complete idiot, supposedly educated, almost a Ph.D. while they talk circles around me . . ." (114).

From May 21, 1948, through June 4, 1948, the diary reveals
the young man's affair with Hilda, a graduate of a famous wom-
en's college in America. They tend to quarrel, even during their
love-making, so that "having sex with her is about the dullest
pastime I can think of. I went to my room and read Tacitus in
Latin, for practice" (117). The American is shocked when a
French acquaintance reveals a penchant for very young boys,
but soon he is confessing to the Frenchman: "I told [him] all
about Jimmy, told him things I myself had nearly forgotten, had
wanted to forget. I told him how it had started at twelve and
gone on, without plan or thought or even acknowledgment until,
at seventeen, I went to the army and he to the Marines and a
quick death. After the army, I met Helen and forgot him completely; his death . . . took with it all memory, a thousand summer days abandoned on a coral island" (121-22). But, despite
his confession, the American is terrified and leaves when asked
to help his French friend when he is arrested at last for his
affairs with young boys.

The final entries in the journal are from the last week in 1953.
By now, the American has given up his studies, settled in New
York to sell antique furniture, and taken his place in the city's
large circles of homosexuals. The American fiancée has married
and lives in Toledo, Ohio; the lady companion in France has
married a designer and lives in San Francisco; and the Frenchman has died, not of opium as expected, but of a malformed
heart. With this entry the journal ends.

CHAPTER 4

The 'Edgewater' Novels

WITH THE PURCHASE of "Edgewater" in 1950, Gore Vidal, just twenty-five that year, both literally and figuratively retreated from the geographic wandering and the literary urgency that had driven him to write six novels in five years. The retreat was soon interrupted, however, by the need to write for hire; but in the two novels that Vidal wrote at "Edgewater" —*The Judgment of Paris* and *Messiah*—he demonstrated the firm control of his medium that had been present in promise more than in execution in his earlier work.

When asked to state his philosophy of life, Vidal once wrote: "I have put nearly everything that I feel into *The Judgment of Paris,* a comedic version, and *Messiah,* a tragic version of my sense of man's curious estate."[1] That estate is one of optimistic uncertainty and of abiding distrust in absolute values of any kind. It is a knowledge that sees man as simultaneously and ultimately all and nothing:

> I can imagine vividly all the millennia when this globe was uninhabited by man and I can imagine with equal equanimity a cold, dusty planet where the race of man has long since perished, his works and days unremembered in that spiraling bright flux we call the universe. The sense of time . . . perhaps the sense of eternity and the unhuman reduces . . . for me the sorrow I might otherwise experience in regarding this race as it now is, incapable of controlling the predatory life force (we live by the displacement of other life). The most that one can . . . that I can do, at least, is to construct my daydreams so that they can perhaps communicate to others my small vision of huge matters which I turn this way and that, taking pleasure in the act of writing. . . .[2]

I   The Judgment of Paris

The best among the eight novels which Vidal published from 1946 to 1954 is *The Judgment of Paris*,[3] a remarkably sound work, written when he was twenty-five. Of great scope and frequent depth, *The Judgment of Paris* is successful because in it the author combines delight in satire and in perfect sentences with several interesting literary conventions. The framework of the novel is a retelling in modern terms of the Greek myth of Paris, who was asked by Zeus to choose the most beautiful of three goddesses—Hera, Athena, and Aphrodite. The hero is an American "innocent" touring Europe to complete his education and to be polished by the older culture, a device found in such works by Henry James as *Daisy Miller* (1879) and *The American* (1887).

Moreover, the style of *The Judgment of Paris* is seemingly appropriated from two nineteenth-century British conventions: as in the brief novels of Thomas Love Peacock, characters are assembled for no other purpose than to talk together interestingly; and, as in the novels of Anthony Trollope, the author addresses his audience in the "dear reader" asides that invite participation in the actual building of plot, character, and theme. These elements are united in a novel that operates successfully on two levels—the serious, on which the story is worked out; and the comic, on which the entire theme is mocked.

Philip Warren, the modern Paris, is enjoying one year of leisure in Europe before he must return to the United States with his vocation and the pattern of his life irrevocably determined. Philip, twenty-eight and handsome, is not very innocent about life after having endured World War II as a junior navy officer and three years in the Harvard Law School. From these years he has a butterfly tatooed on his thigh and a degree in law. About Philip's mind the author confesses: "What sort of man or boy or youth is Philip Warren? Well, it is much too early to draw any conclusions about his character since he is hardly yet revealed" (17). The device used to reveal the hero's character is to have him meet as many diverse "characters" as possible during his year in Europe.

When Philip meets the first woman to tempt him—as Hera, the figure representing power, tempted Paris—he is in Rome, where "the avenue widened and there before him, illuminated

by several floodlights, was the Colosseum, far higher than he'd
ever imagined it to be, solemn in its age. He paused, awaiting
revelation. None came, however . . . he was aware only that his
legs were rather tired from walking and that his left shoe was
pressing too tightly against his little toe" (38). As Philip enjoys
his vision of himself (" . . . he was dedicated to the idea of a
classic detachment and he was wary of any involvement which
might threaten this high cool mood"), Regina Durham speaks
to him in the dark Colosseum. In keeping with the queenly
connotation of her name, Regina is the wife of Rex Durham, the
power behind all American politicians; only a congressman himself, he mysteriously controls all Presidents and lower powers.

When the Durhams try to interest Philip in becoming one of
"their people" by promising him in all seriousness the American
presidency in exchange for merely accepting their control, Philip
becomes Regina's lover; but he scoffs at her political induce-
ments. In describing their love-making, Vidal parodies the various
kinds of pornographers who describe in suggested detail the
whole act of sex:

> Now, to be frank, one hardly knows how far to go in describing
> precisely what happened. There is the brutal school, which uses
> any number of squalid words to get to the point. Then there are
> the incredibly popular lady novelists, who titter and leer, de-
> scribing the hero's great, rough (yet sensitive) hands and the
> back of his bronzed neck (for some unaccountable reason, the
> back of the neck has become, in the male at least, an erotic sym-
> bol of singular fascination). Then there are the sort to whom the
> business is very beautiful and very fine, the center of the book,
> tender and warm and serious, very serious. Much is described,
> as much is left to the imagination. One is moved and, should the
> novelist be a good one, the scene can have a remarkable imme-
> diacy. Yet, in this particular case, at least, we must attempt an-
> other method. For Philip is not brutal nor is the back of his
> neck bronzed nor is he in love with Regina. He finds her attrac-
> tive and desirable and it seems to him like a very pleasant way
> to spend his first night in Rome. (59)

Regina never reveals why she must adopt Philip into her political
plans; she is always serene, controlled, and appropriately passionate, although the affair never becomes love: ". . . now what
he saw he liked dispassionately and he could, he knew, in time

and if all went well, love or at least grow accustomed to her in such a way that he might think himself in love: that grand nineteenth-century passion which had never, at this moment in his life at least, touched him with its burnished wing" (78-79).

While Philip is being tempted by Regina, Vidal introduces his hero to a startling group of background figures who are necessary to his comedy. To illustrate the working of political power on at least one level, Philip meets in Rome a group of royalists who are conspiring to return the House of Savoy to the Italian throne. These are Clyde Norman, "a director of the Fabian Trade Mission, otherwise unidentified"; Lord Glenellen, a British citizen no longer welcome in England because of his "hobbies"; and the two men's royalist, homosexual associates.

Philip, understanding but not sharing in their sexual activities, undertakes a mysterious trip to Amalfi as courier for the group, only to discover on returning to Rome that most of the conspirators have become Communists. In Amalfi he meets two American tourists: "Bella and May Washington were sisters, teachers of English and Social Science, respectively, in the Bigelow Clapp High School of Dubuque, Iowa. Both were unmarried, they hastened to say . . . and both were virginal, he decided, sublimated to a degree that was scarcely human" (99).

And in Capri Philip attends a party given by Zoe Helotius, formerly a peasant but now the incredibly rich widow of a fig merchant. She is famous for knowing, if at all possible, the great men and women of the world: "The vulgarity of Mrs. Helotius was one of the few really perfect, unruined things in Europe; it was a legend and, unlike most highly publicized phenomena, never a disappointment to the eager tourist who (properly sponsored) had got himself into any one of those five villas which decorated the spas of fashionable Europe like rough diamonds, bases for her considerable operations" (122).

Forsaking the company of these interesting people and demanding the exercise of his year's freedom of choice in order to decide on Regina's offer of political power, Philip leaves Italy for Egypt. In *The Judgment of Paris*, Egypt is equated with knowledge, just as Rome is equated with power. The Athena figure who tempts Philip Warren to undertake the intellectual life is Sophia Oliver, who has returned to Luxor to pursue her interests in archeology: "She was handsome, though not pretty in a contemporary sense for her nose was large, like a Julian portrait bust, and her skin was white, unpainted. Yet her eyes were extraordinary, pale gray with long dark lashes, and her hair was a fine auburn, drawn softly back from her face and gathered in a bun at the back. Her figure was good, but he could not tell if she were tall or short. He suspected that she was tall and, though not young, not old either . . ." (171). Sophia is never more closely described: she is meant to be as abstract as the idea of Egypt or as the embodiment of all philosophy that is not demeaned by daily "getting and spending."

Sophia lectures to Philip on the antiquities they journey to see; but his reactions are scarcely those of an intellectual: "Philip, though he liked her, found her positive assertions a little trying; she never spoke tentatively, advanced an opinion as merely an opinion and not a fact of nature. Yet, in general, he agreed with what she had to say and, in any case, he had not yet been in a position to contradict her with a superior knowledge on any subject" (177). Sophia happens to know Regina Durham, whom she dislikes for meddling in the real world of political intrigues. Philip at times wonders at not being sexually attracted to Sophia; he realizes, however, that her reaction to advances would probably be no more than one of quiet amusement.

When Sophia finally invites Philip to join her in intellectual contentment, her terms are so anti-humanistic that Philip has no trouble rejecting them. Sophia advises:

> . . . you should withdraw from what repels you, turn to something that does please you. Music. Ideas. Excellence. Perhaps even the vain schoolboy hunt for "first principles" or, better yet, you like the poetry, not the poet . . . then love the idea which is real, more real than the man who made it, who invented the stories long ago, almost before there were sufficient words to describe the sun and the wind and the earth, love and anger, virtue and wisdom. That's why I have spent my life among the ruins, reading history, learning, avoiding always men and women . . . not that I'm a recluse: far from it, but I never touch them and they never touch me. (199)

The comedic background to the philosophical discussions of Sophia and Philip includes a hotel keeper who speaks an English idiom amalgamated from various cheap American movies;

Mr. Briggs Willys, so rich and fat that he wants only to die; and Mrs. Fay Peabody, American author of innumerable detective novels. When Philip suggests that the master of all criminal behavior help the suffering, fat Willys out of his misery, Mrs. Peabody reluctantly tries to do so. Of course, her ingenious schemes completely fail; and Mr. Willys finally dies voluntarily, having just decided that he probably wants to live.

The Aphrodite figure who tempts Philip Warren to award her the prize of his devotion is Anna Morris, wife of an American businessman who is in Europe to negotiate steel contracts. Although she and Philip first met in Cairo, it is in Paris, traditionally the city of love, that their passion is consummated. Neither the power nor the intellect enjoyed by Regina and Sophia interests Anna. She is really no more than a good lover, the reflection of Philip Warren's *idea* of woman. Her one virtue is not forcing the young man to devote himself to her love.

Having never loved before, Philip yearns for the grand passion that supposedly moves all creation; yet, being a realist, he accepts the individual moments of love as all that he can ever have. Regina admits that her need is for any man who will let her control him, Sophia thinks and lives alone, and Anna accepts intuitively the fact that Philip loves her and will leave her. "Having loved" seems, finally, to be the desirable solution to Philip's problem.

The setting for this decision brings together in Paris most of the comic creations from the scenes in Rome and Egypt. They join characters from Vidal's early novels, who are revived for unexplained reasons: Robert Holton from *In a Yellow Wood* has joined the State Department, Jim Willard from *The City and the Pillar* is now a "kept boy" and drug addict in Paris, and Charles de Cluny from *Dark Green, Bright Red* is wandering around Europe playing courtier. As in Rome, most of the new creations are homosexuals—contented American lovers, rich transvestites, and worshippers of Augustus-Augusta, "the only functioning hermaphrodite in Paris."

Against this comedic background, Philip chooses Anna, as Paris in the Greek myth chose Aphrodite. The decision to devote himself to capturing moments of love is a young man's optimistic solution to the problem of finding a center in life. Considering this solution several years after first publishing *The Judgment of Paris,* Vidal remarked, "I am not at all sure a decade later that I would still give Aphrodite the prize, but my younger self did so without hesitation, and I still honor that commitment."[4]

But the significance of Philip Warren's commitment remains valid, even if the occasion of the choice does not. Given the hypothetically "permanent" choice among power, intellect, and love, only a commitment to love is humanly possible—"humanly" in the sense of "humanistically." For *The Judgment of Paris* is the working out of a devotion to the concept of man as a being more worthwhile in and for himself than as an object of manipulation or abstraction. The idea of the quest is better handled in *The Judgment of Paris* than in *In a Yellow Wood* or *The City and the Pillar,* where the youthful heroes never forego the pleasure of taking their quests seriously. Philip Warren is closer to Blondel in *A Search for the King* in questioning the validity of his quest, or to Peter Nelson from *Dark Green, Bright Red* in seeing the irony in his half-hearted search for meaning.

The Judgment of Paris reads smoothly because Vidal's disquisitions on sex, death, and love seem to belong to the characters who mouth them and because Philip Warren is satirized as thoroughly as he is given sympathy. In other words, Paris is "judged" before the truism that the old gods have not died.

II Messiah

Messiah,[5] the second "Edgewater" novel, is the serious version of Vidal's philosophy and the author's favorite among his ten novels.[6] *Messiah* mingles realism and fantasy, fact and prophecy in order to work out in an imagined future what Vidal believes (at least what in the early 1950's he believed) to be the hidden themes of the present.

In an essay prefatory to *Messiah,* Vidal writes of the early 1950's as a time of uncertainty that was most deeply influenced by "an ill-tempered social philosopher of the nineteenth century" (Marx) and by "an energetic, unreasonably confident mental therapist, also a product of that century's decline" (Freud). In this time of anxiety, all men were aware of the "unidentified flying objects" and other unexplained phenomena that in earlier ages would have been clear omens of portentous happenings. People who may have surmised the truth of these omens in the

1950's did not speak out, for the times crushed nonconformity. When both science and reason were discarded or perverted in favor of emotionalism, there remained only one answer to man's condition:

> . . . in these portentous times, only the scientists were content as they constructed ever more fabulous machines with which to split the invisible kernels of life while the anti-scientific leaped nervously from one absolute to another . . . now rushing to the old for grace, now to the new for salvation, no two of them really agreeing on anything except the need for agreement, for the last knowledge . . . and that, finally, was the prevailing note of the age; since reason had been declared insufficient, only a mystic could provide the answer, only he could mark the boundaries of life with a final authority, inscrutably revealed. It was so perfectly clear. All that was lacking was the man. (21)

The germ for *Messiah* is also to be found in *The Judgment of Paris*. In the Egyptian episodes of *The Judgment of Paris*, when Philip Warren is being tempted by Sophia Oliver, the Athena figure, she expresses her belief in the following prediction made by an Arabian prophet:

> The world is an evil place today, more evil than ever before. The men kill each other with machines and the women go without veils and act like men in the streets and bazaars, while both men and women have deserted the faith and the angel of Allah stands at the gate of heaven looking down upon the earth, ready to blow the trumpet which will put out the sun and shake the stars out of the night and level the mountains, the cities in a sea of flame. But the angel's moment has not come for a new token of Allah's mercy has appeared in a land to the west, a village by the sea. He will grow up a holy man and he will teach the word of Allah to all the world. The people shall hold him in reverence and call him saviour for he will teach them not to fear death. (206)

When Sophia truly believes that this messiah will come, Philip remarks: "That would be the end" (200).

Messiah utilizes the honored literary convention of the fictitious memoir: an old man records just before dying not only the story of a movement in which he took part, years ago, but his present need for writing this history. Eugene Luther is an

American who has lived in Luxor, Egypt, for many years. He has sought exile among the Arabs in order to escape from the new religion which he had helped spread in the United States late in the 1950's.

Luther remembers his first meeting with Iris Mortimer, a serene, cultured woman of some beauty, at the home of Clarissa Lessing, his neighbor in the Hudson Valley. Luther, a middle-aged esthete, has independent wealth and philosophical tastes. Clarissa, a mysterious socialite, convincingly claims to have lived for thousands of years and to have known most of the great men in history. Luther and Iris become friends at Clarissa's urging, neither of them knowing "the mythic roles" that their friendship would assume.

Iris has become intrigued by "a kind of preacher" in California. Clarissa manages to have Luther accompany Iris to hear a sermon by the new evangelist. In some degree a hypnotist, John Cave is able to command attention and belief in his one tenet: he has the absolute knowledge that "death is good." Formerly an undertaker's assistant, Cave claims no divine inspiration or religious "angle"—just the knowledge that man should not fear death, the complete end to the unhappiness of life. Suicide and even gratuitous murder are good.

Luther gradually accepts Cave's assertions because he welcomes any philosophy that releases men from fearing death so that they can love life. Iris devotes herself to Cave, Clarissa maneuvers Luther into forming a corporation, and "Cavesword" is spread across the United States by films, speeches, and television. Cave gradually assumes a secondary role in the new religion when Paul Himmell, an advertising expert, assumes control of the Cavite movement.

In only a few months, there are thousands of converts to Cavesword, in spite of Christian opposition and governmental investigations. Luther writes books and publishes a Cavite newspaper, Iris and Cave train hundreds of evangelists, Paul uses all the propaganda devices available to advertising, and Clarissa mysteriously controls the whole movement. When the doctrine of death takes effect, there are thousands of suicides in America. Because "death is good," man has no fear of dying—and no reason to live.

Unfortunately for Cavesword, Eugene Luther, who at first seized upon the doctrine as an expression of faith in human life, becomes disenchanted with the religion of death. With the entire nation now Cavite and with the movement spreading across Europe and South America, Luther tries to halt the emphasis on suicide by insisting that John Cave practice his own faith and die. Cave is very much opposed to dying; but Paul, realizing that Cavesword must have a dead founder in order to live, kills Cave. The founder dead, Iris assumes control of the religion and chooses to emphasize suicide instead of life without fear of death. But she helps Eugene Luther escape from the Cavite extremists who consider his humanism a heresy.

As with any myth, *Messiah* reads infinitely better than it summarizes. Vidal chronicles very carefully the steps by which Cavesword becomes an almost universal religion, and he is careful to present Cavesway (suicide) as one desirable attitude toward the problem of human existence. The old man in Egypt feels compelled to record the true origins of the religion in the West; for, as he learns from an American "communicator" sent to convert the Arabs in Egypt, the movement has spread its tenet throughout all the world but the Near East. Using the powers of medicine and psychiatry, Cavesword has reduced life to total, forced conformity.

There are many intriguing points to *Messiah*. The novel can be read as an allegory of the growth of Christianity. John Cave can be Jesus Christ, discoverer of the knowledge that death is not to be feared. Paul Himmell can represent Saint Paul, who may have perverted or adapted the original messiah's words to suit his own needs. Iris, who really directs the movement after Cave's death, becomes venerated as Cave's spiritual "mother." And Eugene Luther can represent Martin Luther, whose reforms redirected part of Christianity into Protestantism.

However, the presence of Clarissa in *Messiah* raises the novel to another plane of meaning. She is clearly a witch figure, an eternal intriguer in human affairs. It is Clarissa who considers Cavesword "a plot" that she can enjoy perpetrating against humanity. Clarissa introduces Iris, mythically the messenger of the Greek gods, and (by association with Isis, the Egyptian goddess) a symbol of motherhood, to Eugene Luther, whose name happens to be the first and second names of Gore Vidal! But in *Messiah* Eugene Luther, because of some unspecified physical or mental infirmity, is unable to consummate his unconfessed love for Iris Mortimer, whose last name suggests the Latin word for "death."

This interpretation is not meant to suggest, however, that *Messiah* is Gore Vidal's fictionalized account of his defeat of a personal death wish. But surely the novel must operate as more than a satire on the American cliché "It can't happen here" or as a sophisticated imitation of George Orwell's *1984* (1948) or of Aldous Huxley's *Brave New World* (1932). Eugene Luther, having embraced Cavesword for its positive value in freeing man from the tyranny of death, becomes the moralist of Cavite, Incorporated. With absolute ethical power in his hands, he decrees that marriage and family life are to be discouraged. Any restraints upon personal freedom of action are to be removed. Although his laws are only vaguely presented in *Messiah*, those laws markedly resemble the ethical statements of the author.

But Cavesword turns against this rather vague humanism and chooses to persecute heretics, correct deviationists, and enforce conformity to the unthinking mediocrity so easily fitted over the human race. The old man recording this story is a "non-person," one who has been written out of Cavite history except for his name; the few who deviate from Cavesword are still called "Lutherists."

Messiah ends with Luther's recollection of what John Cave, the new messiah, whispered as he died: "Gene was right." That is to say, Cave realized that the way of death could not be the way of life. The old man writes, just before dying: "I shall not take Cavesway even though I die in pain and confusion. Anubis [the Egyptian god of the tombs] must wait for me in the valley until the last and, even then, I shall struggle in his arms for I know now that life, *my* life was more valuable than I knew, more significant and virtuous than the other's was in her [Iris'] bleak victory" (254). The human race may be destined for self-destruction (it is surely destined for cosmic destruction), but the individual human can by intellectual action make his own life exempt from the racial suicide wish.

Eugene Luther's last words in *Messiah* reveal *him* as the true messiah, one who, ironically, was unaware of his "mission" when he could have effected its message: "Though my memory is going from me rapidly, the meaning is clear and unmistakable and I see the pattern whole at last, marked in giant strokes upon the air: I was he whom the world awaited. I was that figure, that messiah whose work might have been the world's delight, and liberation. But the villain death once more undid me and to *him* belongs the moment's triumph. Yet life continues, though I do not. Time bends upon itself. The morning breaks. Now I will stop for it is day" (254).

CHAPTER 5

In Gentlest Heresy

GORE VIDAL confesses readily that he is not at heart a playwright. He is

> a novelist turned temporary adventurer. . . . The reasons for my conversion to piracy are to me poignant, and to students of our society perhaps significant. If I may recall in nostalgic terms the near past, I did, as a novelist, enjoy a bright notoriety after the Second World War. Those were the happy years when a new era in our letters was everywhere proclaimed; we would have, it was thought, a literature to celebrate the new American empire; our writers would reflect our glory and complement the beautiful hardness of our currency. But something went wrong.[1]

The "error" was the refusal of the public to buy enough of his books to give him a decent living, for "by the 1950's I and my once golden peers were plunged into that dim cellar of literature characterized as 'serious' where, like the priests of a shattered establishment, we were left to tend our prose privately, so many exiles, growing mushrooms in the dark."[2] Turning to the theater for money, Vidal found that the New York City audience was, to say the least, a discouraging one:

> It is a middle-aged, expense-account audience, suffering from the bourgeois *malaise* so well diagnosed by Sartre when he remarked that the middle class will endure any sort of shock or discouraging statement about the human conditions as long as the author makes it perfectly clear that no change is possible. For change is the enemy, reminding the audience not only of revolution and the loss of money, but finally (and most secretly) of death. For a social meliorist like myself, the Broadway audience present a tricky problem: how to get them to recognize certain flaws in our society (and possible reforms) without openly antagonizing them.[3]

Vidal has not taken to the theater any illusions about the extent of his dramatic talents. As a playwright, he is "a sport, whose only serious interest is the subversion of a society that bores and appalls me. . . ."[4] With no interest in the future of any play, Vidal cares less about the well-made play than about the well-unsettled audience: ". . . what I have done, and what interests me, is to clown, to be funny, bizarre—and I enjoy comedic invention, both high and low, there is almost nothing so satisfying as making an audience laugh while removing their insides."[5] Audiences have enjoyed two of Vidal's plays—*Visit to a Small Planet* and *The Best Man*. But they have been dubious about one of his dramas, *On the March to the Sea*, and actually hostile to another, *Romulus*.

I Visit to a Small Planet

Vidal's first full-length drama, *Visit to a Small Planet*,[6] is the most humorous of his four published plays. The first version of *Visit to a Small Planet* was presented as a one-hour television drama on May 8, 1955. The success of this version encouraged Vidal to develop the brief television script for commercial production in New York City, where, in 1957, the play enjoyed a long season, one followed by success in Europe and by adaptation into a film.

Vidal accepts the criticism that *Visit* is more an entertainment or vaudeville than a regular drama: ". . . the comedic approach to the theme tended to dictate the form. Having no real commitment to the theatre, no profound convictions about the well-made or the ill-made play, I tend to write as an audience, an easily bored audience. I wrote the sort of piece I should like to go to a theatre to see: one in which people say and do things that make me laugh. And though monsters lurk beneath the surface, their presence is sensed rather than dramatically revealed."[7]

The action of *Visit to a Small Planet* takes place between one summer evening and the next in the home of Roger Spelding, outside Manassas, Virginia. Spelding is "a confident middle-aged man with a receding hairline and an odd double manner: when he is being a television commentator, he is warm, folksy, his accent faintly Southern; when he is himself, the accent is more national, the tone more acerb and sophisticated" (9). As the play opens, Spelding is talking with General Tom Powers, "an adept politician of the services, devoted to his own advancement, which has not been as rapid as he'd anticipated. He ascribes all set-backs to treachery in high places" (9). Powers complains volubly over having been taken away from "the new Laundry Project—something really exciting" to handle an alleged Unidentified Flying Object seen over the Virginia countryside for the past twelve hours. When Powers insists that the object is really there, Spelding's first worry is that he has just taped a news analysis for television in which he has told "Mother and Father America that there 'jest ain't no sech animal.'"

Reba Spelding, "a vague grey woman, beneath whose gentleness glints the iron will of the faddist," welcomes her husband's old friend, although her main concern at the moment is whether her daughter Ellen—to the consternation of the Speldings—is sleeping with Conrad, a young neighboring farmer who is more interested in agriculture than in money making. Conrad is "an ordinary-looking youth, more earnest than serious," and Ellen is "a splendid girl of nineteen, iron-willed but appealing." Their main concern is daring to check bravely into motels; at the last one Conrad signed the register as "Mr. and Mrs. Ulysses Simpson Grant *and wife*." As they are planning to carry a suitcase filled with telephone books to a motel that night, and as Reba Spelding is locating a pamphlet on birth-control for her daughter, the flying saucer lands in the family's rose garden.

The occupant of the vehicle is Kreton, "a visitor from outer space . . . a pleasant-looking man with side whiskers . . . dressed in the fashion of 1860." Kreton, who came to earth to view the Battle of Bull Run at Manassas in 1861, is mistakenly a century late. He is on a pleasure trip, "a visit to your small planet. I've been studying you for ages. In fact, one might say you're a hobby of mine . . . especially this period of your development" (24). Reba pragmatically invites Kreton to stay for dinner, and General Powers takes over the house to question the alien and to fill out the necessary forms (in quadruplicate) for the Pentagon.

General Powers, anxious to guard the security of his country, considers Kreton "a spy sent here by an alien race to study us, preparatory to invasion": "We'll fight them with everything we've got. We'll fight them with the hydrogen bomb, with poison gas, with broken beer-bottles if necessary; we'll fight them on the

beaches; we'll fight them in the alley . . ." (28). Kreton, able
to hear people's thoughts, delights in the general's "vibrations."
The authorities, however, are not soothed by the visitor's insistence that he has come alone and that "no one would ever dream
of visiting *you!* Except me. But then, of course, I'm a hobbyist.
I love to gad about" (29). The government becomes especially
upset at Kreton's announcement that he loves earthmen so deeply
that he is taking control of the planet, of his "dear *wicked* children," and that "tomorrow will be a wonderful day for all of us."

Act II opens the next morning with Kreton and the family cat
telepathically discussing dogs, mice, and the delights of being
feline. Vidal originally opened this act with a conversation between Kreton and the Secretary-General of the United Nations,
but the subject—war—disturbed the audiences: "At each performance the audience, which had been charmed by the prece-
dent fooling, grew deathly cold as the debate began: this was
not what they had anticipated (a fault, I own, of the dramaturgy),
and their confidence in the play was never entirely regained. . . .
The substitute was engaging; the play moved amiably; no one
was shocked."[8]

Knowing Ellen's passion for Conrad, Kreton regrets having
upset their plans: "You had planned to devote all of last night
to wild abandon, you and Conrad and the four telephone books.
How glorious you must be! Tangled in one another's arms, looking up telephone numbers. . . . I suppose that's what you *were*
planning to do with those books. So bizarre, the whole thing"
(41). Unable to understand their objections to his urgent request
to watch them at play, he raves over "these primitive taboos.
You revel in public slaughter: you pay to watch two men hit
one another repeatedly, yet you make love secretly, guiltily and
with remorse . . . too delicious!" (42). On Kreton's world, there
is no passion at all; people have become "intergalactic bores."
To escape this boredom, Kreton has visited earth, where he enjoys "absolutely wallowing in the twentieth century."

But the twentieth century—at least in the United States—de-
cides that Kreton would be the perfect weapon in possible international warfare. Unfortunately, war is Kreton's mania; he has
begun maneuvering Russia and the United States into such
mutual suspicion that nuclear warfare is imminent: "I simply
dote on people. . . . Why? Because of their primitive addiction

to violence, because they seethe with emotions which I find bracing and intoxicating. For countless ages I have studied them and now I'm here to experience them first-hand, to wallow shamelessly in their steaming emotions . . . and to have fun, fun, fun! . . . How? . . . Well, I do believe I have started a war. At least, I hope so. After all, that's what I came down here to see! I mean, it's the one thing they do really well" (52).

Dressed as a Confederate general, Kreton is prepared to enjoy the disaster. He tries to arouse war fever in Conrad, who prefers sex and agriculture to war, by singing the patriotic songs guaranteed to motivate savages to bloodthirst. When this motivation fails, he cleverly gets Conrad, a sensible pacifist, to fight a soldier attracted to Ellen; for even Conrad is primitive when he is properly stimulated: "Savages, blood-thirsty savages. That's why you're my hobby. That's why I've returned to the Dark Ages of an insignificant planet in a minor system circling a small and rather chilly sun to enjoy myself, to see you at your most typical . . ." (73).

In Act III, Vidal averts nuclear warfare with a *deus ex machina* ending for his play. Ellen, having been taught some slightly advanced mental tricks by Kreton, telepathically calls for aid to prevent the war; and another visitor arrives—Delton 4. He stops the war by "bending" time back to earth's pre-Kreton hours, explaining that Kreton "is a rarity among us. He is morally retarded and, like a child, he regards this world as his plaything . . ." (78). Kreton goes into space to return to his "nursery"; and the play closes—time bent back—as the first lines of Act I are repeated.

This stage play is an improvement over the earlier television script of *Visit*. The love antics of Ellen and Conrad, the delightful loquaciousness (rather than dire threats) of Kreton, and the visitor-cat interview are fortunate additions. However, Vidal admits to having tailored his script to protect the investments made in his play; it was obviously better to produce a play that would be popularly successful and mildly satirical than one that would be mildly successful and bitterly satirical: "I was obliged to protect an eighty-thousand-dollar investment and I confess freely that I obscured meanings, softened blows, humbly turned wrath aside, emerging, as we all wanted, with a successful play which represents me very little. It is not that what was fashioned is bad or corrupt. I rather fancy the farce we ended up with, and I think it has a good deal of wear in it. But the play that might have been, though hardly earth-shaking, was far more interesting and true. I played the game stolidly according to rules I abhor."⁹

In the guise of this science-fiction fable, Vidal manages to entertain the reader or the audience with vaudeville tricks—mind-reading, weird sounds, teleportation—and to satirize some of the ridiculous aspects of American society in the 1950's: nationalism, patriotism, sexual hypocrisy, the military mind, nuclear warfare, and birth control. A painfully funny play, *Visit to a Small Planet* reflects Vidal's interest in immediate world problems and his conviction that only direct action can give man even a slight chance of surviving self-destruction: "My view of reality is not sanguine and the play for all its blitheness turns toward a cold night."¹⁰

II The Best Man

Vidal's second full-length drama, *The Best Man*,¹¹ opened in New York City in March, 1960, and became even more successful than his earlier *Visit to a Small Planet*. The year 1960 was a fortunate time to present a play about politics because Vidal was then a candidate for Congress and because the United States was to hold a Presidential election in November, 1960. *The Best Man* concerns the national conventions held by the American political parties to select candidates for the Presidency. It is strange that the inspiration for this political satire came to him from his consideration of the narrative method of Henry James: ". . . I wonder if, really, I am taken with James's way. Is he too neat? Too artificial? Too classical? Too much devoted to balance? Item: *The Tragic Muse*. Each of four characters begins at the farthest extremity of an X; they cross; each ends in an opposite position. One wonders, does a living pulse beat? Or is it only a metronome?"¹²

Deciding that he did not like the sterile neatness of James's plot, Vidal imagined how a modern writer might use the method:

It was all a trick, an easy parlour-game. As if one were, in contemporary terms, to take—just for example—a man of exemplary private life, yet monstrous public life, and contrast him to a man of "immoral" private life and exemplary public life. That was

just the sort of thing James would do. How he would enjoy me-
chanically turning the screw upon each character. For the sake of
argument, make the two men politicians, perhaps fighting one
another for the Presidency. Then demonstrate how, in our confused age, morality means, simply, sex found out. To most Americans, cheating, character-assassination, hypocrisy, self-seeking
are taken as the way things are, not pleasant perhaps but: son
you've got to look after number one because there's a lot of com-
petition and . . . I had the characters for *The Best Man.*[13]

With the characters established, Vidal decided to set his play
at the nominating convention held in Philadelphia by an unnamed American political party. The scenes alternate between
action in the hotel suite of candidate William Russell and in
that of his opponent, Joe Cantwell. As the play opens, Russell
is the favored contender at the convention. Russell, "a strong
youthful-looking man of fifty" and formerly a Secretary of State,
is aided in his campaign by his manager, Dick Jenson, "in his
late forties: intense, devoted, apprehensive by nature," and by
his wife, Alice, "in her early forties . . . a handsome, slender,
grey-haired lady of the Old Establishment, not quite as diffident
and shy as she appears."

Russell is a caricature of the very clever, rather pompous intellectual who, knowing his own great wit, enjoys using it to
the confusion of less clever men. Asked how many delegates he
has "sewed up," Russell replies: "When it comes to delegates,
we neither sow nor do we reap" (160). He refuses to speculate
on a "dark horse" candidate, saying: "I'm sorry, but I'm not
about to build up a dark horse when I'm doing my best to look
like the light horse" (161). Russell subjects even newspaper re-
porters to a statement of his political creed: ". . . life is not a
popularity contest; neither is politics. The important thing for
any government is educating the people about issues, *not* following the ups and downs of popular opinion. . . . If the people
want the wrong thing, if the people don't understand an issue,
if they've been misled by the press . . . —by *some* of the press—
then I think a President should ignore their opinion and try to
convince them that his way is the right way" (161). He alludes
to Oliver Cromwell, William Shakespeare, and Bertrand Russell
and then ends the interview with the old cliché—source of the
title of the play—"may the best man win!"

Russell promises his worried aide that he will resist impulses to refer to Charles Darwin and all ancient Romans, but he admits to being unable to pass a mirror without regarding his reflection and to studying the future in multiples of three. However, his more serious concerns are whether American women will vote for a man not only intelligent but also promiscuous and whether everybody will learn of his unhappy marriage to Alice. The women's vote is supposed to be represented by Mrs. Sue-Ellen Gamadge, who not only dislikes wit ("eggheads") and all first ladies since Grace Coolidge but who warns Russell that his opponent plans to use "smear tactics" in the campaign.

Alice Russell is helping her husband in the campaign by pretending that their marriage is conventionally happy. Her motives are unclear even to herself: "I want to be First Lady. Or perhaps I look forward to seeing you occasionally. . . . Don't look alarmed! Only in line of duty. You know, an unexpected meeting in the East Room, an ambiguous encounter in the Lincoln Bedroom . . ." (171). Sadly aware of her husband's promiscuity, Alice worries that the public will learn of Russell's past nervous breakdown—obviously the "smear" the opponent will use.

Joe Cantwell, the opponent, "is in his forties. His manner is warm, plausible. Though under great tension, he suggests ease. He has a tendency not to listen when preoccupied" (181). For public support, Cantwell relies on his senatorial investigations of organized crime, on his clean image, and on his pose as the average American, equal to his countrymen but in no way superior to them. His marriage to Mabel Cantwell, "a blond, pretty woman of forty," is a happy one in the mindless American way of mediocrity, except that in private Joe and Mabel revert to their usual baby talk; they play Papa and Momma Bear. Cantwell tailors his statements to parallel the opinions of the majority of voters, he needs the support of ex-President Hockstader, and he plans to ruin his opponent by revealing Russell's psychiatric record.

Cantwell threatens to publicize Russell's nervous breakdown because, as Vidal says, "The *Zeitgeist* is full now of the buzz of psychoanalysis; everyone's mind is cluttered with at least a few misunderstood clinical phrases and conceptions. If William Russell had once had a nervous breakdown, and Senator Cantwell were to get his hands on Russell's case history and threaten to reveal the contents to the delegates at the convention, it was unlikely Russell could survive politically. A presidential candidate can have many faults, but even a hint of mental instability is disqualifying."[14] Hockstader, who has really planned to back Cantwell as nominee, changes his mind at the threat, telling Cantwell: "It's not that I mind your bein' a bastard, don't get me wrong there. . . . It's your bein' such a stupid bastard I object to" (193).

Russell, suspecting Cantwell's tactics, is planning a public statement from his doctor; but his manager has found a method of countering Cantwell's threats. Vidal explains the countermeasures thus:

> What could be brought up about Senator Cantwell? I wanted something ambiguous: it might or it might not be true but, true or not, Russell must resent having to reveal it, even to save himself. This was limiting. If Cantwell had stolen money, got a girl pregnant, run away in battle, taken dope, been a Communist or a member of the Ku Klux Klan, Russell might be reluctant to bring the matter up, but he would certainly not hesitate to save himself, especially if he were convinced the charges were true. Homosexuality was about the only thing left. It was a charge which, true or not, Russell would detest exploiting.[15]

The evidence for Cantwell's supposed degeneracy rests on statements volunteered by Sheldon Marcus, his fellow officer during World War II when they had served in the Aleutian Islands. Cantwell rather plausibly denies the charges as vengeance for not having promoted Marcus and explains his role as having been an official spy on a circle of homosexual soldiers. Hockstader personally does not care "if Joe Cantwell enjoys deflowering sheep by the light of a full moon," but he forces Russell to confront Cantwell with the charges. But Cantwell, knowing his opponent's distaste for the whole matter, bluffs successfully and releases Russell's psychiatric profile to the delegates.

The issues established, Vidal brings *The Best Man* quickly to a close. Russell withholds his charges; Cantwell makes his charges public; and Hockstader dies, saying "to hell with both you." When neither candidate can get a majority of votes from the delegates, Russell ends his own chances and prevents Cantwell's nomination by giving his support to a political unknown, "a man without a face": "Don't underestimate him. Men without faces tend to get elected President, and power or responsibility or honour fill in the features, usually pretty well" (238). A safe man nominated, evil having canceled out good, Vidal commits a distasteful dramatic impropriety by letting Russell and his wife decide to try for a reconciliation; Russell is, "of course, happy: the best man won!"

The Best Man seems to be the author's comment on some aspects of American politics: "the best man" may be neither the ruthless opportunist nor the gentle intellectual but rather a man of no public renown—a compromise candidate. Of course, the play operates on hyperbole and simplification. It assumes that the two secrets would have been kept hidden in an otherwise open society, that the candidates themselves would do the dirty work, and that the nominee would become President in spite of opposition by the other political party. To all attempts to allegorize his drama, Vidal replies: "Contrary to rumor, I was not writing about Adlai Stevenson, Richard Nixon and Harry Truman. There were elements of these men in each of the characters, but no more. At a crucial moment in our history I wanted to present to an audience of voters a small essay in Presidential temperament."[16]

The Best Man is probably his most topical play and, therefore, quite easily dated in its appeal and comprehensibility. The success of the performances in 1960 was due not only to the impending Presidential election but to Vidal's changing the script to suit the audience, as he had done earlier with the script of *Visit to a Small Planet:*

In the play's first version, I allowed the opportunist Senator Cantwell to win. The good man was too weak, the bad one too tough. The play was black and I was willing to fight to keep it so (and enjoy almost certain popular failure) if I had been entirely convinced that a man as bad as Senator Cantwell could get elected. After much thought I changed my mind. Cantwell could not prevail—at least nowadays—because in its idiot way our system, though it usually keeps us from having the very best man as President, does protect us from the very worst. That is two cheers for democracy.[17]

III   On the March to the Sea

On the March to the Sea[18] is another expansion of a television script into a full-length drama. According to Vidal, "the play began as an hour drama produced on television in 1956. I called it *Honor*[19] and in that form it was, generally, successful. The story was very American: a businessman named Hinks imbues his sons with a lofty rhetorical notion of honour and duty which does ennoble them; yet when he himself is put to the test, he fails, but in his failure discovers that he has never in his heart believed his own cant."[20] The play based on this script has never been performed in New York City, although it was acted in Bonn, Germany, in 1961, and in summer stock at Hyde Park, New York, in 1960. *On the March to the Sea* has been reworked by Gore Vidal several times; but as published in *Three Plays*, it remains the least successful of his four dramas.

On the March to the Sea, set in Waynesville, Georgia, in 1863-1864, is a drama of the American Civil War. John Hinks, the protagonist, is "a powerfully built man in his late forties, rough of speech, vigorous in manner; he limps stiffly; one leg is false but he uses no stick" (90). The limp dates from an accident in Hinks's youth, when he was a homeless orphan befriended by Mr. Grayson, in whose mill Hinks was injured. Having envied Grayson and other members of the aristocratic gentry of the ante-bellum South, Hinks has worked hard enough to achieve wealth comparable to theirs; and he has adopted their code of honor. As the play opens, Hinks is celebrating his achievement of equality with the landed gentry; he has just finished building a great plantation home on his own extensive estate.

This first party in the new house is Hinks's opportunity to entertain his son Grayson, home on leave from the battles in the Northern states of the Confederacy. Grayson pretends to share the ideals of the South, but he has survived enough battles to know that "honor" is hollow on a battlefield and that the South has in reality never had a chance to win the war. Grayson's main concern is that his younger brother, Aaron, a student at the university, will not enter the army. Grayson realizes that the South will need men like Aaron to rebuild civilization after the war is lost.

Aaron himself wishes to avoid entering the service; he is a sensible boy, silently peaceful and mainly interested in marrying Amelia Blair, daughter of aristocratic neighbors. Before Aaron can announce his plan to marry the pregnant Amelia, Hinks forces him to accept "with honor" a commission in the Confederate Army. The sons are to fight together to defend the South and their father's new mansion: ". . . these things come down on us like storms in summer and who is right and who is wrong is maybe impossible to judge. But what matters is what you *do*, whether it is to offer your life like Grayson here, or me goin' broke sellin' grain below cost to my state. It is what you *do* that makes you what you are, not what you say, not even what you think. It is what you do in the world. The thing you *have* to do because something tells you inside: that is honour" (103).

Seven months later, the Northern Army is near Hinks's new home. He has volunteered to lead his neighbors in burning all their homes to prevent the Yankees from using or looting them —the "honorable thing to do." There has been no news of either of his sons, but defeat has not lessened Hinks's business sense: he generously pays the worthless Confederate money to his friends in exchange for land sold in their despair. But, when Union soldiers requisition his house for quarters, Hinks is constitutionally unable to burn his own home. The businessman in him defeats the pretension to gentility and honor.

Hinks is contrasted to Colonel Thayer, leader of the Union troops. A contractor and architect in peacetime, Thayer describes himself as "just an ordinary innocent killer of men." He does *his* duty as a soldier, although he hates himself for so easily being a barbarian and destroying life and property: ". . . in all conscience, don't tempt me to hurt you. . . . Because I want so much to be cruel. Do you hear that? Do you know what it is to revel in destruction? To delight in the pain of others? Oh, it is ravishing to be cruel and I confess it! If only you knew how gladly I would burn this house and you and the whole earth if I could get it in my hands! Do you hear that? I am drunk with cruelty and I hate it even as I love it and I beg you . . . please . . . help me and save yourself . . . help me and save me, too!" (120). Aware of the business sense in Hinks, Thayer preserves the house to quarter his officers before they "march to the sea."

A week later, the officers are planning to give themselves a party in Hinks's home to celebrate leaving to join in the siege of Atlanta. The townspeople hate Hinks for not burning his house and for seeming to cooperate with the Yankees. Amelia Blair, now obviously pregnant, appears just in time to learn from a letter intercepted by Thayer that Grayson is missing in action and that Aaron is dead. She and Mrs. Hinks realize that Aaron has been sacrificed to his father's inconsistent sense of duty and honor.

While the officers enjoy their party upstairs, Grayson surreptitiously visits his parents. He berates his father's selfishness and false sense of duty—the cause of Aaron's particularly horrible death (he lay wounded and unattended between the lines for two days, unable even to kill himself). When Hinks tries to keep Grayson from leaving to rejoin the Confederate Army, Grayson insists on doing his duty, for Hinks's sons have taken seriously their father's cant about "honor." They have become what he wanted, while he has revealed his hypocrisy in wanting what they have become. As Grayson leaves, disgusted with his father, Hinks set fire to his fine home—to the admiration of Colonel Thayer!

There are several rather obvious flaws in *On the March to the Sea*. Each of the characters except Thayer is a stereotype from the romantic American versions of the Civil War: Grayson, the chivalric son and bravely defeatist soldier; Amelia, the aristocratic but strong girl; Mrs. Hinks, the simple-minded wife in silent subservience to her husband; and Hinks, who is no more than one of William Faulkner's Snopeses achieving some self-awareness. Aaron, the only intelligent Southerner in the play, could have been given more significance as a pacifist in wartime instead of being shuffled off the stage, an easy victim of his father's pride. And Thayer's function as a sympathetic foil to Hinks is confused when the Northerner is given the role of philosophic sadist and commentator on the effect of war on otherwise "decent men."

Finally, there is doubt over the meaning that Vidal assigns to Hinks's final act. Burning the house is not an acceptable "offering" for having encouraged one's sons to die uselessly; it resembles too closely the "happy ending" school of drama. Arthur Miller's *Death of a Salesman* (1948), a play remarkably similar to *On the March to the Sea*, demonstrates the quality missing in

Vidal's dénouement—irony. Willy Loman's suicide is both noble and useless, but Hinks's new self-knowledge seems to insist on his nobility—in a play that (in the character of Thayer and in the words of Grayson) explodes the whole myth of nobility and "honor." According to Vidal, "Hinks is the self-made man, the opportunist, the brigand founder of a dynasty, an embodiment of the life force . . . or a traitor, depending on one's own point of view, and that is where my failure began."[21]

However, resolving the uncertainty over Hinks's character would not necessarily improve this play. Because the cast of characters is stock and the theme is trite, *On the March to the Sea* should wisely be left in print but not put upon the stage.

IV Romulus

Vidal first wrote in 1959 of the work of Friedrich Duerrenmatt, the Swiss dramatist and novelist, who happened to attract his attention just when he had decided that "Love" as the universal panacea operative in every American play had become reprehensible to him: "But, now, like an avalanche in far-off mountains, comes Friedrich Duerrenmatt, a Swiss detective story writer with a genius for the theater, to give us a new theme, or rather to remind us of an ancient one: justice. And he has arraigned with wit our Loving time before that austere tribunal."[22] The two writers met, and Vidal arranged to adapt Duerrenmatt's *Romulus der Grosse* for presentation in New York City, although the play had failed in Germany, France, and England.

Thinking that he could make *Romulus der Grosse* interesting enough to succeed in the United States, Vidal justified the practice of adapting another man's play by invoking the names of such adapters as William Shakespeare, André Gide, Albert Camus, Tennessee Williams, Thornton Wilder, and Arthur Miller. He then decided that Duerrenmatt's play "was undramatic"[23] because the theme was stated too early and then merely repeated for four scenes and because the characters were classical rather than Shakespearean. One other change, and the adaptation was done—Vidal added many topical jokes:

> True comedy uses everything. It is sharp; it is topical; it does not worry about its own dignity; it merely mocks the false dignity of others. Aristophanes did not write to be great in eternity. He wrote to influence the life of his day. He used every kind of

joke he could think of, and many of them concerned people sitting in his own audience, references often unfathomable to us now. But Aristophanes endures because of his engagement in the vulgar life of his own time. *Romulus* in its way is equally a speaking picture of some of our day's follies and foibles.[24]

Romulus takes place from March 15 to March 16, A.D. 476. The last Emperor of the Roman Empire, named for the legendary founder of Rome, is a quiet chicken farmer who stays at his Tivoli villa and does not worry about the state of the Empire, rapidly being conquered by the armies of Ottaker the Goth. Romulus is the negligent husband of the Empress Julia, who married him because, being the daughter of a slave, she needed a patrician husband in order to become Empress. They have a daughter, Rea—formally engaged to Aemillian, for years a captive of the Goths—who usually conducts herself as though she were acting in one of the classical tragedies which she studies. There are courtiers who consider themselves the last preservers of world order and bureaucrats who know that good governing is done on paper. Not far away the Goths battle the last Roman army— and win.

Romulus knows that he is ruling in the last days of the Roman Empire. A former professor of history, he should know how to govern well; but his policy has been one of non-government. Romulus has judged the past and decided that the guilt of Rome's history must be expiated in its present:

> *I* did not betray Rome. Rome betrayed herself. Long ago. Rome knew truth, but chose power. Rome knew humaneness, but chose tyranny. Rome debased herself, as well as those she governed.
> . . . This throne is set upon a mountain of empty grinning skulls, streams of blood gush upon the steps to this high place where Caesar sits, where *I* sit, presiding over those cataracts of blood which are the source of power. . . . Rome is old and weak and staggering, but her debt is not yet paid, nor her crimes forgotten. But the hour of judgment is near. The old tree is dying. The ax is ready. The Goths have come. We who have bled others must now ourselves be bled. You have asked for justice. I shall give it! I sentence Rome to death! (61)

The Emperor ignores entreaties to "save the state" from "the international menace of Gothic-ism." He feeds his chickens, named for former emperors and for Ottaker (the most productive hen of all). When Julia and the bureaucrats try to move the government to Sicily, all are drowned; the Byzantine emperor pleads for asylum; and Otto Rupf offers to save the Empire.

Rupf, dressed suggestively like a modern international businessman, is a manufacturer of pants, the new garment worn by the Goths and, therefore, the style of the future. He thought first of buying the Empire, but its precarious financial state dissuaded him. In exchange for marriage to Rea, Rupf will now *pay* the Goths to withdraw from the Empire instead of conquering it. Romulus, who rejects the offer, encourages Rea and Aemillian, escaped from a Gothic prison, to marry and be happy—in other words, to forget a dying empire and to accentuate the human. They, too, drown.

Romulus is almost assassinated (by everyone in Tivoli) before he can carry out his plan of dissolving a moribund empire, but he survives to meet Ottaker, fearsome ruler of the Goths. Ottaker, to Romulus' surprise, is himself a chicken farmer—and a warlord because his subjects, dressed as modern German soldiers, force him to lead them in battle. Ottaker wishes to prevent the future militarism of the Germans; Romulus wishes to expiate the sins of Rome's militaristic past. Knowing that they must both fail, the two rulers agree to survive in peace: to "act as if all the accounts in the world were finally balanced, as though spirit had finally triumphed over matter" (78).

This little intellectual comedy could not possibly have flattered audiences accustomed to serious discussions of world war and world peace and to idealized faith in their political leaders. Surely, one should not joke about patriotism, militarism, and the "patterns of world history"! And New York audiences did rebel at the ironic idea of justice. Vidal recalls, "I used to listen to the odd laughter at *Romulus*. It would begin after a line the audience thought funny; then it would die in the throat and there would be a half gasp . . . what *are* they saying? Can it be that we are not loved in this house, but judged? I put the case more strongly than the play warrants. Romulus was more good-humored than not."[25]

The humor in *Romulus* may be gentle and good, but behind it is Vidal's knowledge (apparently shared by Duerrenmatt) that "I and my race are nothing in eternity. . . . I know we shall not endure. The present is all time."[26]

CHAPTER 6

A New Sun, Another Day

IT WAS PROBABLY both inevitable and desirable that when Vidal began to write fiction again late in the 1950's, his subjects would be less autobiographical, less personal, and more "public." The novelist Louis Auchincloss writes shrewdly of Vidal: "He knows at first hand what the struggle for power amounts to and what it does to men. One might go so far as to suggest it his primary interest in life."[1] Vidal corroborates this statement of his theme by concerning himself in "how the society works, even on the most pedestrian level—the politics of it. . . . Politics meaning how people make a society work, how we get on with one another."[2] To demonstrate what people will do to achieve power over one another, he has written his most recent novels about the Roman Empire and about Washington, D.C.

I Julian

Eugene Luther, the narrator in *Messiah,* confessed to having an "eccentric purpose which, for some years, had been the study of history in a minor key" (26). Luther was reading about the Emperor Julian and planning to write about him when the reading was done, although "there is so much of interest to read that it seems a waste of time and energy to write anything . . ." (34). Later in *Messiah,* Luther confesses:

> I had got almost nowhere with my life of Julian. I had become discouraged with his personality though his actual writings continued to delight me. As it so often happens in history I had found it difficult really to get at him: the human attractive part of Julian was undone for me by those bleak errors in deed and judgment which depressed me even though they derived most logically from the man and his time: that fatal wedding which finally walls off figures of earlier ages from the present, keeping them strange despite the most intense and imaginative recreation. (54)

Gore Vidal is not the first writer to be intrigued by the Roman emperor who tried to give complete religious tolerance to Rome and thus to history. After the millennium of the Dark Ages, during which Julian was *The* Apostate, humanists of the early modern period began writing of Julian as a personality instead of anti-Christ. Michel de Montaigne, Baron de Montesquieu, Voltaire, Denis Diderot, Edward Gibbon, and Alfred de Vigny can be named as admirers and defenders of Julian. In 1873, Henrik Ibsen published *Emperor and Galilean,* a very unhistorical drama that is just as well unknown because it is so dull. In 1895, Dmitri Merezhkovski published *The Death of the Gods,* the first novel to deal with Julian. Then, lamented a classicist, "Julian has once more been taken over by the scholars, as in the Middle Ages," because "no man of letters in the 20th century has taken up Julian where the 19th left off."[3]

In 1962, Vidal published two trial chapters (written in 1959) of a new novel on Julian with the following note:

> I vowed virtuously that all historical detail should be accurate. As a result, it took five years of reading to master the contemporary source material; then, spokes to my central figure, I started to study the books *he* studied, to read about the men and the places he knew. The thing threatened to become endless. Arbitrarily, I stopped reading and began to write. . . I do hope to finish this work one day, for so much of what we are not (and might have been) was decided during the life of this philosopher-king. . . .[4]

Having mastered the three volumes of Julian's own writings and the six classical accounts of the emperor's life, Vidal had to read about the fourth century itself: "I became more and more at home in the fourth century, and to do a man's life, it is necessary to know the time perhaps better than the man, because the character you create will be a work of your own imagination and that is why, paradoxically, one must not be free with facts. By remaining absolutely accurate in detail, one can invent a good deal in spirit."[5] Detail and spirit coalesced, and *Julian*[6] became Vidal's ninth novel.

The framework of *Julian,* one used previously in *Messiah,* is the tested device of the fictitious memoir that is edited with comment. However, the author shapes the device by pretending that the memoir was not published at all (the emperor's memoir has *not* survived), but that the manuscript itself and comment appended to it are reproduced as a novel, along with letters between the original editor and an associate. *Julian* is, therefore, a fictional autobiography of the emperor, amplified by fictional notes and letters written by Libanius of Antioch and Priscus of Athens, friends of Julian. Libanius was a renowned writer of letters—two thousand of them survive—and Priscus was a historical person whose writings are not extant.

Julian opens with Libanius' writing to Priscus in A.D. March, 380: "Yesterday morning as I was about to enter the lecture hall, I was stopped by a Christian student who asked me in a voice eager with malice, 'Have you heard about the Emperor Theodosius?'" Theodosius has decreed that "the days of toleration are over"—that no longer can non-Christians expect to live in peace in the Roman Empire. Libanius has a scholarly plan to counteract this edict:

> Seventeen years ago when you returned from Persia, you told me that our beloved friend and pupil, the Emperor Julian, had written a fragment of memoir which you had got hold of at the time of his death. I have often thought to write you for a copy, simply for my own edification. I realized then, as did you, that publication was out of the question, popular though Julian was and still is, even though his work to restore the true gods has been undone. Under the Emperors Valentinian and Valens we had to be politic and cautious if we were to be allowed to go on teaching. But now in the light of this new edict, I say: an end to caution! We have nothing but two old bodies to lose, while there is eternal glory to be gained by publishing Julian's memoir, with an appropriate biography to be written by either or both of us. (5)

Priscus replies to Libanius' request by agreeing to furnish a copy of the manuscript (not gratis) and to help in the editing, but he fears being associated with the work:

> . . . if Theodosius did permit a biography, it would have to avoid the religious issue. The bishops would see to that. And for ferocity there is nothing on earth to equal a Christian hunting "heresy," as they call any opinion contrary to their own. Especially confident are they on that subject where they are as ignorant as the rest of mankind. I mean death. Anyway, I don't

want to fight them, because I am one and they are many. And though I am, as you so comfortingly suggest, old and near the end of my life, I enjoy amazingly good health. I am told that I look no different than I did at forty, and I am still capable of the sexual act at almost any time. (7-8)

After considerable epistolary bantering between the two scholars, Vidal opens Julian's memoir with the following words: "From the example of my uncle the Emperor Constantine, called the Great, who died when I was six years old, I learned that it is dangerous to side with any party of the Galileans, for they mean to overthrow and veil those things that are truly holy" (15).

It slowly emerges that Julian Augustus is leading his armies into Persia to fight King Sapor. Fearing that he may not survive the campaign, the emperor is dictating his memoirs. He writes matter of factly about his birth in 331, about the murder of his father by the Emperor Constantius, and about his precarious survival under a very suspicious, frightened emperor. Young Julian and his older half-brother Gallus were royal heirs to Constantine and, therefore, theoretically dangerous pretenders to the throne of the Roman Empire.

According to Julian, he and Gallus survived childhood only because Constantius could have no children and wished to preserve the lineage of Constantine. Childhood over, the young men would have to plot their own survival and never appear to challenge the throne of Constantius. Julian has never accepted Constantine's conversion to Christianity: "Constantine was never a a true Galilean; he merely used Christianity to extend his dominion over the world. He was a shrewd professional soldier, badly educated and not in the least interested in philosophy, though some perverse taste in him was hugely satisfied by doctrinal disputes; the mad haggling of bishops fascinated him" (17).

Under the Christian teachers assigned to guard Julian and Gallus, Julian remembers pretending piety and total acceptance of Christian doctrine; even as a child, he secretly deplored the Christians who murdered and hated one another in the name of a God of "love." Gallus trains to become a soldier; Julian pretends to study for the Christian priesthood: "Let Gallus shine. I preferred obscurity and survival" (45).

As a young boy, Julian has his first "true" religious experience.

In a dream, someone calls his name, and "then—I don't know how—but I realized that it was the sun who had spoken. Huge and gold above the city, the sun reached out fiery arms to me. And with an astonishingly poignant sense of coming home, I plunged straight into the blazing light. And awakened to find that the setting sun was shining in my face. Dazzled, I got to my feet. I had been overwhelmed by light. I was also bewildered. Something important had happened. But what? I told no one about this vision" (26).

Later but similar experiences convince Julian that he is chosen by Helios, God of the Sun, to restore worship of the old Greek gods. Sosipatra, a spiritual medium, and Maximus, a magician, assure the young man that he is destined to become emperor and to worship rightly. He goes through various pagan "mysteries" and learns pagan theology—all done secretly while pretending devout Christianity. Priscus interrupts Julian's memoir to comment: "But like so many others nowadays, poor Julian wanted to believe that man's life is profoundly more significant than it is. His sickness was the sickness of an age. We want so much not to be extinguished at the end that we will go to any length to make conjurer-tricks for one another simply to obscure the bitter, secret knowledge that it is our fate not to be. If Maximus hadn't stolen Julian from us, the bishops would have got him. I am sure of that. At heart he was a Christian mystic gone wrong" (78-79).

Constantius lets Julian become Caesar and sends him to Gaul to recapture areas lost to the Germanic barbarians. Julian, knowing nothing of warfare, proves himself a born soldier and fights as victoriously as his ancestor Julius Caesar. He pretends never to think of desiring to be emperor; but the Gallic soldiers, refusing to fight for Constantius, proclaim him Julian Augustus.

Julian does not style himself Augustus. All too clearly, however, he has expected circumstances (and his gods) to force him to accept the throne. Only close friends, among them Priscus and Libanius, know that Julian intends to regard the office of emperor as a divine appointment for returning religious equality to the empire. Just before Julian and Constantius meet to fight, Julian receives a fortuitous letter: "I read the first line. Then the words blurred together and I could read no more. 'Constantius is dead.' As I said those extraordinary words, the clerks one by one fell to their knees. Then, as in a dream, the room began to fill with people. All knew what had happened. All paid me silent homage for I had, miraculously, with the stopping of one man's breath, become sole Augustus, Emperor of Rome, Lord of the world. To my astonishment, I wept" (287).

On December 11, 361, Julian enters Constantinople as emperor. He forces a few unwilling soldiers to worship pagan gods and tries to be a continent, reasonable, devout ruler. The Christian bishops are properly horrified at Julian's religious decree that no person is to be persecuted for belief, non-belief, or worship of any god—as long as violence is avoided. The Christians thrive on violence and hatred; it is they who name Julian "Apostate." Julian, really kind to his Christian subjects, assures them:

> . . . you have nothing to fear from me as Pontifex Maximus, *if* you behave with propriety and obey the civil laws and conduct your disputes without resorting, as you have in the past, to fire and the knife. Preach only the Nazarene's words and we shall be able to live with one another. But of course you are not content with those few words. You add new things daily. You nibble at Hellenism, you appropriate our holy days, our ceremonies, all in the name of a Jew who knew them not. . . . But I am not here to criticize you, only to ask you to keep the peace and never to forget that the greatness of our world was the gift of other gods and a different, more subtle philosophy, reflecting the variety in nature. (338)

Now at the pinnacle of earthly power, Julian is ripe for decline. The two agents attending, if not instigating, that decline are Maximus, the magician who rules the Emperor's spiritual life, and Ormisda, exiled heir to the throne of Persia. Ormisda assures Julian that Persia can be defeated in battle, and Maximus assures the Emperor: "You are Alexander." Level-headed Priscus comments that "From certain things Julian let slip during the Persian campaign I did get the impression that he believed he was in some spectacular way supported by the gods, but I had no idea that he actually thought he was Alexander, or at least had the ghost of Alexander tucked inside of him. . . . This particular madness explains a good deal about the last stages of that campaign when Julian-Alexander began to act very peculiarly indeed" (347).

Madly ambitious to extend the Roman Empire from Britain to

India, Julian invades Persia; and, although he wins battles, he cannot conquer a people who prefer to burn their crops and flee than to surrender. Despite warnings from the omens which he so often consults and rumors of assassination plans among his Christian officers, Julian unwisely moves so far into Persia that only through retreat can he save himself and his men. In a minor skirmish with Persian cavalry, he is stabbed with a Roman spear and dies, refusing to speak of the weapon or to name a successor. With Julian's death, at thirty-two, on June 25, 363, no obstacle prevented an intolerant Christianity from overwhelming the Western world. Libanius concludes *Julian* with these words:

> I have been reading Plotinus all evening. He has the power to soothe me; and I find his sadness comforting. Even when he writes: "Life here with the things of earth is a sinking, a defeat, a failing of the wing." The wing has indeed failed. One sinks. Defeat is certain. Even as I write these lines, the lamp wick sputters to an end, and the pool of light in which I sit contracts. Soon the room will be dark. One has always feared that death would be like this. But what else is there? With Julian, the light went, and now nothing remains but to let the darkness come, and hope for a new sun and another day, born of time's mystery and man's love of light. (502)

Vidal's narrative is accelerated and more narrowly focused just before Julian's death by a slight change in the framework of the novel. Julian ends his memoirs and resorts to brief, military notes in a journal about the Persian campaign. Priscus now interprets and comments on this journal; at Julian's death, it was he who stole both memoir and journal. It is through Priscus that Vidal fixes blame for the emperor's assassination.

His curiosity newly aroused by Libanius' interest in Julian's death, Priscus visits the emperor's servant, who had been with him in battle in Persia and who is now a very rich man. Callistus has prospered inordinately under several emperors and bishops. He confesses the reason: ". . . it was I who killed the emperor Julian." Priscus comments: "There it is. The end of the mystery. Callistus regards himself as one of the world's unique heroes, the unsung savior of Christianity" (493).

Julian owes at least half its success to the comedic invention of Priscus and Libanius. Their personal spites and jealousies are not dulled by advanced age, and the two scholars are clearly differentiated. Libanius is a devout pagan and a member of one of the mystery cults; he is scandalized at Priscus' mockery of the mysteries. To Priscus' joy in his own continuing sexual prowess, Libanius expresses fastidious abhorrence. Libanius is always too ready to defend Julian's deeds; Priscus sees all life as essentially useless, death as the end of man's curious charade, and Julian as the misguided victim of lesser men.

However, Priscus and Libanius are thematically more important as a petty chorus that corrects and amplifies Julian's memories of his strange career. Vidal explains his device:

> I had . . . the problem of verisimilitude. I wanted to give not just the usual report in the first person by your historical principle, but I wanted to put up at least two mirrors to study it; so I picked these two ancient philosophers, some years after his death, trying to show that at times Julian is clearly lying and also the two old men, each in his own way is also distorting a point which will perhaps never be clear. And I thought that struck me as a rather useful way to show that to come at the literal truth of anything is extremely difficult. And the more mirrors in which you can see any event obviously the more interesting, to my mind.[7]

Julian Augustus, seen from three perspectives, is the most complex character that Vidal has created in his novels and plays. The final effect of *Julian* is that of a modern, civilized man trying to understand the last civilized man of the ancient world. To Vidal, Julian was "a passionate high-brow. The new testament seemed to him a barbarous, uneducated work, in much the same way a sermon by Billy Graham might strike the ear of a Harvard professor of philosophy."[8]

Although Julian was a military genius and a sensible administrator, his religious beliefs seem to fascinate Vidal: "I find Julian an engaging and a good man, even though his own religious views were very peculiar, to say the least. He loved magic, believed in omens, tried to organize every superstition and rite into one grand Hellenic church, and of course he failed. But had he lived, there is no doubt that Christianity would have been but one of several religions in the West. And this diversity might have saved the world considerable anguish."[9] If the virtue of Julian's life was his insistence that religious absolutism is dangerous to the human spirit, then the vice of it was "that he tried to counter it, by reorganizing every single mystery cult and becoming bull-burner as he was known because of his burnt offerings."[10]

Yet Vidal's larger interest is the consequences of the fourth century for modern civilization:

> . . . without some understanding of what happened then, it is impossible to have a clear idea of what Christianity is and how it came into being. And if we do not understand Christianity, then we cannot make much sense of the world we live in, because our society, morally and intellectually, for good and ill, is the result of that great force. At a series of ecumenical councils during Julian's lifetime, the trinity was invented as well as the doctrine of the holy ghost and the beginnings of the cult of Mary. All these things were hammered out in a series of stormy conventions, and there was much violence. In fact, the murderous instincts of Christian absolutism first emerged in the fourth century. And I do not think it an exaggeration to say that over the centuries, Christianity has been responsible for more bloodshed than any other force in western life."[11]

Had Julian not been murdered, what would his reign have been like, according to Vidal? "Stormy. But had he reigned for thirty years, I have no doubt but that Christianity, despite its absolute tendencies, would have been but one of several religious sects in the west, and not necessarily dominant. Just because the church has endured such a long time does not mean that it was inevitable. Nothing is."[12] But Julian died; Christianity prevailed; the barbarians conquered Rome. Vidal's ultimate point is that "we should never forget that we are the descendants of the barbarians, but not yet civilized."[13]

II Washington, D.C.

Although the United States is a nation whose literary artists have customarily disdained politics and politicians, it has produced a considerable number of political novels. Private and public corruption in Washington, D.C., especially has fascinated American novelists: the condition of Washington must reflect in microcosm the condition of the nation. Among notable American political novels—usually written to condemn the politicians and their policies—are Henry Adams' *Democracy* (1880), Hamlin Garland's *A Spoil of Office* (1897), David Graham Phillips' *The Plum Tree* (1905), Frances Hodgson Burnett's *Through One Administration* (1914), John Dos Passos' *The Good Design* (1949), and William L. Shirer's *Stranger Come Home* (1954). Gore Vidal, having written as his tenth novel a traditional examination of Washington politics, called his work simply *Washington, D.C.*[14]

Vidal begins his story on July 22, 1937, on a stormy night in a tempestuous political season. Peter Sanford, sixteen, walks in the rain and darkness to watch his sister Enid make love in the family poolhouse. Peter's father, Blaise Sanford, who owns the most important newspaper in Washington, D.C., is celebrating a major legislative defeat of President Franklin D. Roosevelt, whose liberal politics offend Blaise and Senator Burden Day. Senator Day is an "honorable" legislator, one who enjoys manipulating political power but whose goal is really to serve well the constituents who elected him. Blaise Sanford himself cannot rise to greater personal power; he is looking for a younger man to support and to guide to the Presidency.

That man cannot be his son Peter, who is as yet only a rich but thoughtful playboy. Vidal uses Peter Sanford as his own voice in *Washington, D.C.*, although the lives of the author and his persona are not very similar. Episodes devoted to Peter's growing awareness of his adult role (and notice of his increasing girth) regularly mark Vidal's chronicle of life in Washington from 1937 to around 1954.

The foil to Peter is Clay Overbury, legislative assistant to Senator Day. Clay is too poor to do more than learn from his admired employer how to survive politically: "Early on, he had observed that most ambitious young men tend to gravitate to those who already have power; and though this was natural and necessary, too often in the process they neglected those who did not yet have power—like themselves—but some day would. Clay liked to think of himself as one who planned ahead . . . he spun himself a wide web of relationships, just in case" (42). To achieve at once power and wealth, Clay rejects his boss's daughter and elopes with Enid Sanford, whose wealthy father immediately disowns his new son-in-law. Blaise is not yet ready to adopt Clay as his political instrument.

Meanwhile, Senator Day, usually very honest, accepts a bribe from an oil speculator in order to finance his campaign for the Presidential nomination in 1940. Clay secretly files away knowledge of this indiscretion for his own future use. Day analyzes his assistant thus:

> Clay was always practical and Burden wondered if he believed in anything at all. It had been his experience that, contrary to legend, young men are seldom idealistic. They want the prizes, and to rise they will do whatever needs doing, echoing faithfully the rhetoric of the day. Idealism comes later in life, if ever. After all, politics was largely twisting and turning merely to survive, and in the process even the simplest goal was lost sight of. Disgust with one's own kind was inevitable while eternity mocked them all. (75)

The outbreak of World War II ruins Day's chance for the Presidency; Roosevelt announces that he will campaign for a third term. But the war is the great opportunity for Clay Overbury, who accepts a commission and deliberately seeks to emerge from battle as a hero—a giant step toward a great office for himself. Peter Sanford manages to spend the war years at a Pentagon job; Enid, now very promiscuous, separates from her adulterous husband; and Senator Day recovers from a serious stroke suffered at the home of his mistress.

The second half of the novel concentrates on the rise of Clay Overbury, finally leagued with his father-in-law in search of power. Blaise's newspaper builds Clay into a national war hero so that he can easily enter the House of Representatives when the war is over. The death in combat, meanwhile, of a former companion startles Peter Sanford into accepting an adult role:

> The time of drifting was at an end. The years in school and in the Army were all so much time forever wasted. Now he must put a stop to the drift. . . . He would do this thing for its own sake, like Scotty, who had died doing something which, in the moment's frame at lest, was meaningful. But that was maudlin, he

told himself severely, and not true. To die for any thing was just as bad as to die for nothing. He had meant to survive the war and he had survived. Now he must pay the price for this sensible caution and use his life properly. (201)

Peter and Senator Day's daughter publish *The American Idea,* a sophisticated liberal magazine. And they become casual lovers. The war almost over, President Roosevelt dies and thus deprives Senator Day of any victory in the continuous Senate-White House struggle. Clay returns to civilian life, ready to pursue Blaise Sanford's dream of political power in an altered world:

Clay thought he understood the shape of this new world. In any case, he did not regret the passing of the old America, unlike Burden, who truly believed his own rhetoric and was moved by his own sentimentality. Burden wanted to bring to all of those without the law that sense of common dignity which was, he believed, America's peculiar gift to the world. But to Clay there was no dignity of any kind in the race of man, nor was the United States anything more than just another power whose turn at empire had come, and in that empire he meant to wield power entirely for its own sake. In this he resembled not Burden, the flawed idealist, but the old President who had prevailed by mingling cant with shrewdness in such a way as to inspire his followers and confuse his enemies none of whom quite realized what he was up to until, by dying, it was suddenly plain to all but the totally deluded that the author of the Four Freedoms had managed by force of arms and sly maneuvering to transform an isolationist republic into what no doubt would be the last empire on earth. (243)

Clay and Blaise exercise power to destroy Enid in order to protect Clay's career; Enid's crime was to suggest that Blaise's attraction for Clay was unnatural. She escapes from her asylum and dies in a car wreck. Peter's attempts to avenge his dead sister quickly close the novel. When Peter reveals the lie behind Clay's heroic legend, Clay remembers Enid's confession of adolescent incest with her brother. Clay reveals Senator Day's one dishonest act—taking the bribe in the late 1930's. Clay becomes a senator at the time when Senator Joseph McCarthy is conducting his anti-Communism investigations:

So far none realized that Clay's dim record was the result not so much of an unzealous temperament as of a conviction that at this moment in the Republic's history the people wanted only to be let alone to watch television and forget the exhausting trials of the recent war. To offer them adventure in their current mood would be disastrous. Later, if required, thunder might roll, lightning flash; and Clay had perfect confidence that when the time came he could make whatever weather the bright days of his primacy required. (304)

Peter's exposé having failed to defeat Clay, Senator Burden Day, out of place in this new world, dies. Peter ends *Washington, D.C.* by assuming a love for Diana Day:

. . . he was often able in her company to forget for long moments what he knew to be the human case: that the generations of man come and go and are in eternity no more than bacteria upon a luminous slide, and the fall of a republic or the rise of an empire —so significant to those involved—are not detectable upon the slide even were there an interested eye to behold that steadily proliferating species which would either end in time or, with luck, become something else, since change is the nature of life, and its hope. (376-77)

One does not need more information about the action of *Washington, D.C.* to notice that Vidal has reused a startling amount of material from his previous books. Almost every work in the canon contributes a situation or an idea. For example, *The Season of Comfort* gives the themes of sibling incest, reactionaries disliking Franklin Roosevelt, liberals building the United Nations, the hero's homosexual childhood lover who dies in World War II, and adultery as the Washington way of life. *The City and the Pillar* donates the homosexual lovers, the hero's decision to become vital to life, and the philosophy of mutability. *The Judgment of Paris* presents a scheming female social climber, various homosexuals, and a hero seeking a purpose. Of the dramas, *The Best Man* demonstrates deceitful and adulterous politicians as well as political bribery, "faceless" leaders, and the threat of disclosed homosexuality; and *On the March to the Sea* pictures the "honorable" man who is unable to survive in a new age.

But these earlier works have no hint of the style of *Washington,*

D.C., which is like the lucid prose of *Julian* but more studiedly dispassionate. Not a word is incongruous, misplaced, or super-fluous; this is consonant with the narrative technique, which is conventionally chronological, each chapter being centered around a major event from 1937 to 1954. The large number of characters (who illustrate rather than directly represent the panorama) are kept perfectly controlled by the author's centering his plot around two young men—Peter Sanford and Clay Overbury.

Vidal says of his tenth novel: "I don't think *D.C.* is much like anything I've done before. Obviously it retraces some of the material used—or misused—in *Season*, but in its attempt to 'say it all,' I can't think of any earlier book that much resembles it. The style is deliberately plain at many points, and very clear and precise . . . for me. The book went through more versions than any of its predecessors, and I think the tone is right for what I wanted."[15]

What Gore Vidal wanted to do in *Washington, D.C.* was to chronicle the meaning of the world in which he matured. "No writer has had my luck," he comments, "to be born in the place, class, time that I was, and the bad luck to be so much absorbed by public business."[16] Fascinated with a society that bores and appalls him, Vidal illustrates in *Washington, D.C.* how one man can live in that imperfect society: he can assume that his in-tegrity is valuable to at least himself, that a moral man can sur-vive intellectually in an immoral society.

Thus *Washington, D.C.*, a "summary novel," is technically an almost flawless book, although the "love-the-answer" ending is unfortunate. Published when Vidal was forty-two—a young age —the success of the novel should encourage him to write beyond technical perfection and toward the genius that should not be stifled. That genius liberated, Gore Vidal should write better books.

CHAPTER 7

Interim Reports

G ORE VIDAL has deserved a better hearing from literary critics than he has received. A group of curious factors has influenced the course of his critical reputation: youth, frequent publication, financial success, being a "public person," and using traditionally forbidden subject matter. None of these factors should affect critical judgment of a literary work; but, in Vidal's case, critics stand strongly condemned—for cowardice.

I *The Reports*

Until Vidal published *The City and the Pillar*, his novels had enjoyed considerable praise. True, the praise for *Williwaw* was mixed with wonder that the author was only twenty. However, Jonathan Daniels called the novel "a wholly masculine story of hard drinking and hard work, of all the varieties of fear, of homesickness, vanity and courage" and concluded: "But this is definitely not merely another book about war experiences. It is a novel of great promise by a young man whose skill as a craftsman is more important than his service as a soldier."[1] Another critic wrote of *Williwaw* as a work showing "little strain and lots of discipline."[2]

In a Yellow Wood was better received than most second novels. Nathan L. Rothman called it "a first-rate example of controlled naturalism. It looks easy, but I should say it is a product of concentrated workmanship, a rigid and painstaking selection of details plus a delicacy of statement that reaps its delicacy of tone. The impression . . . is that every word tells, and has been considered for its significance. It is a small work, of marked talent."[3] Stephen Stepanchev had high regard for *In a Yellow Wood:*

> The novel demonstrates Mr. Vidal's psychological astuteness. It shows, too, that the author has a good eye for metropolitan surfaces and an accurate ear for ordinary speech. The dialogue is never strained or stilted. In fact, the book reads well throughout. But its special virtue is its admirable structure. Mr. Vidal has produced a neat, logical, carefully integrated story. He clearly intends every action, and the end is implicit in the beginning. The novel has none of the sprawl and looseness that one generally associates with the work of a beginner.[4]

Then came *The City and the Pillar,* a book that Vidal has never expressed regret about writing. For eight weeks early in 1949, the novel was listed in the *New York Times* as a best seller, and it has remained in print since its first publication in 1948. However, a discussion of *The City and the Pillar,* published by the influential *New York Times Book Review,* set an unfortunate example for most other reviewers of the work: "Presented as the case history of a standard homosexual, this novel adds little that is new to a groaning shelf. Mr. Vidal's approach is coldly clinical . . . he has produced a novel as sterile as its protagonist."[5] *The New Yorker* called the novel "the kind of dreary information that accumulates on a metropolitan police blotter. Artistically it represents the latest, and possibly ultimate, stage in the decline of the literature of homosexuality to the level of unadorned tabloid writing."[6]

A more intelligent critic praised the novel for being "frank, shocking, sensational, penetrating and exhortive."[7] *The Saturday Review of Literature* commended the author "for his realism and honesty"[8] and connected the novel by suggestion to another best seller—*Sexual Behavior in the Human Male* by Alfred Kinsey *et al.*[9] In this connection, J. S. Shrike criticized *The City and the Pillar,* along with the Kinsey report and Truman Capote's *Other Voices, Other Rooms.*[10] Shrike praised Vidal's new novel for avoiding the pseudo-Gothic inventions of Capote and for corroborating in its subject matter the findings of the Kinsey survey.[11]

Unfortunately, it was not these words of praise but the words of the *New York Times* which, as Vidal remarks,

. . . popped up to haunt that book, and all my writing ever since: "clinical" and "sterile." "Clinical" is used whenever one writes of relationships which are not familiar—I dare say that if the story had dealt with a boy and a girl instead of two boys the book would have been characterized as "lyrical." "Sterile" is an even deadlier curse upon the house, and comes from a dark syllogism in the American *Zeitgeist:* the homosexual act does not produce children therefore it is sterile; Mr. X's book is concerned with the homosexual act therefore the book is sterile.[12]

Had Vidal written a succession of novels closely imitative of *The City and the Pillar,* he would have enjoyed no worse reviews after 1948 than those elicited by his "experimental novels." Evaluating *The Season of Comfort,* William Weaver wrote of "a complete absence of anything honestly interesting" and wondered "what seemed good about Vidal's earlier books, since this one is so unrelieveably bad."[13] Leo Lerman called *A Search for the King* "a private whim, the fulfillment of a too personal daydream";[14] and *Dark Green, Bright Red* deserved the unfavorable reception that it received. Richard Match found the novel lacking in significance or point of view,[15] and R. D. Charques found the author "by no means without talent, though his is as yet an immaturity that might thrive better without publication."[16] At this low point in Vidal's critical esteem, John Aldridge published his *After the Lost Generation.*[17]

When Aldridge first wrote about Vidal in 1947, he had great praise for *In a Yellow Wood* as being representative of the novels of the "New Generation."[18] Soon after *The City and the Pillar* appeared, Aldridge wrote in "America's Young Novelists: Uneasy Inheritors of a Revolution"[19] that this work "represents a distinct gain for Vidal" and added: "When one considers that Vidal has succeeded not merely in putting futility behind him but in making a tragic affirmation in the midst of futility, his achievement becomes impressive indeed." However, by 1949, Aldridge was expressing doubt about Vidal's achievement: "I have said that Vidal's attempt to discover the sensibility of the age has so far been only partially successful. 'The Season of Comfort,' like 'The City and the Pillar,' represents another phase in his struggle. In both novels, Vidal has tried to grasp issues that are of first importance to us and to his generation, only to fall short of them through a failure of his technique to draw their full meaning into his material."[20]

In *After the Lost Generation,* Aldridge expanded these ideas of "futility" and "issues of importance" in order to declare that *Williwaw* and *In a Yellow Wood,* both of which he had previously admired, were artistic failures because the author "needed a point of view, a set of values through which he could make his theme dramatically meaningful. But the emptiness that is behind these first two novels makes it clear that he never had them, that, in fact, the search of his characters for a spiritual center is really the shadow of his own private search for an artistic center of meaning."[21] When Aldridge wrote of the "sterile" homosexual relationships in *The City and the Pillar,* he finally stated the central criterion of his criticism:

> . . . when we have explored all the flaws of the novel we have still not really arrived at the basis of its total failure, which is that it is at bottom a thoroughly amoral book—not *immoral* in the conventional sense, because it deals with homosexuality, but amoral in the purely ethical sense, because there is no vitality or significance in the view of life which has gone into it. It seems to have evolved out of an absolute spiritual nothingness in which all things suffer from the same poverty of content and in which the vitally important and the cheaply trivial are viewed alike. If Vidal showed signs in his previous work of a weakening of his technical and dramatic power, he here shows the far more disturbing signs of a spreading rigidity of soul.[22]

Aldridge concluded the discussion of Vidal in *After the Lost Generation* by considering him "typical of his generation. He has lived through some of the most crucial events of history. He has read all the books, listened to all the psychiatrists, and been thoroughly purged of dogma and prejudice. The experience has left him with one thing which it is sheer suicide for a writer to learn too well—that all things are relative and that there are at least twenty sides to every question."[23]

This criticism of literature according to the presence or absence of "absolute values" has influenced tremendously the reception given Vidal's work in both mass media and the academic community.[24] The early 1950's were not favorable toward nonconformity, relative values, or amorality. As a result, Aldridge's criticism sounded right to a decade that needed absolute values or reassurance about the values it considered absolute. So, charged with amorality and artistic sterility, Vidal's two really sound novels of the 1950's—*The Judgment of Paris* and *Messiah*—went almost unnoticed and unbought; and the writer abandoned the novel for his season of piracy.

This nadir in Vidal's critical image in the 1950's is clearly illustrated in the reception given to *A Thirsty Evil* in 1957, when, as he says, "I was not only out of fashion but any writer who dealt with homosexuality could count on a particularly rabid press."[25] The *New York Herald Tribune* accused him of "cynical sophistication and ironic worldliness,"[26] and the *New York Times* added in chorus: "Students of what used to be called 'abnormal' psychology may be interested in these bleak, essentially clinical commentaries: it is highly unlikely that they will attract more sophisticated readers. There is acute perception here, and sensitivity, and effective irony, but Mr. Vidal's stories lack illumination; the atmosphere is as murky as that of a den."[27] Even the *New Republic* renewed the old charge of "sterility": ". . . to a certain extent Mr. Vidal himself appears to dwell in a private realm, attending only fitfully to the world at large."[28]

Had Vidal not at this point become a successful dramatist, he might never have revived his reputation as a novelist. Marya Mannes wrote most understandingly of *Visit to a Small Planet:* "The play is pervaded by such good humor and speeded by such inventive stage business that a number of genuine satirical pricks are gone almost before they draw blood. Almost. For although Mr. Vidal has gone nowhere near as far with his initial idea as a real social critic could, he has managed to kid, if not the pants, then the socks off a number of precious American concepts. . . ."[29] And *The Best Man* prompted Max Ascoli to ask: "Can irony and fantasy once more be made to play a role in the public appreciation of current politics? Can it really be that political satire is finding a foothold on the stage? At least it is happening now thanks to Gore Vidal. . . ."[30]

With Vidal's reputation thus established for wit, satire, and irony and with the popular success of *Julian* in 1964 and *Washington, D.C.* in 1967, his reputation as a novelist was revived. *Julian,* widely advertised as the author's first novel in a decade, remained for thirty-two weeks on the *New York Times* list of best-selling fiction. This popularity is puzzling, for most critics claimed to be confused by the character of Julian. Rex Warner praised the comedic invention but concluded about the emperor: "It is much to Vidal's credit that he has imparted some life to this enigma, but the enigma still remains."[31] Walter Allen appreciated the complexity of Julian's character: "Julian, as we find him in Gore Vidal's recreation, is not anything so simple as the last of the Pagans. He is fatally contaminated by the very factors in the psyche that gave rise to Christianity itself. He is man in an age of transition, looking back to the past, tugged whether he likes it or not into the future by forces he cannot control. It is this, as Vidal well shows by implication, that gives him his universality and makes him emblematic of man in our own time."[32] "Emblematic of man in our own time"—perhaps these words explain the nature of what Gore Vidal has tried to be in his writing.

II *The Achievement*

Surely, Americans have learned by now not to expect an apocalypse in their literature. The most that they can confidently expect is that some among them are going to live and learn— and write. And out of the slag-heap of published writing there will come many books that are competently written and a few books that are extremely well-written. The well-written books may be the least popular of all, but the nation cannot claim a sophisticated literati until a proper measure of appreciation is given to all its authors who see clearly and say well.

The serious novel *is* doubtless now following poetry into that land of aridity and analysis where literature is cultivated in splendid academic isolation. The fact may sadden its devotees, but it should cause them at the same time to look about and praise where praise is due. When words of this praise are bestowed, Gore Vidal will be recognized for speaking to his age in several voices. His voices have not always resounded clearly because he is still very actively a part of the age—an era that could do well to listen and then evaluate.

The first voice of Vidal is that of a former literary prince who has survived lionization and subsequent banishment. "Eight novels in eight years and still only twenty-nine years old!" Therein lie enough charges for banishment; but what of those eight novels, from *Williwaw* in 1946 through *Messiah* in 1954? Were they really worth any attention at all?

The heroes of these early novels, after the gray-gloomy soldiers of *Williwaw*, are young men who seem to be no more than mirrors to reflect what they see so clearly but understand so vaguely. In six novels, Vidal's protagonists are handsome, conventionally educated, taut-bellied but not muscle-bound fellows who move among stockbrokers (*In a Yellow Wood*), homosexuals (*The City and the Pillar*), Washington politicians (*The Season of Comfort*), medieval crusaders (*A Search for the King*), mercenary revolutionists (*Dark Green, Bright Red*), and tired European socialites (*The Judgment of Paris*). They are young men in search of life-centers, of worthwhile objects that promise final stabilization. Some among them settle on business, love, or power as temporary sustainers. The more unfortunate, who take these superficialities as absolutes, ironically are destroyed in their safe harbors; the wiser ones recognize that the quest is irrevocable once begun and that any safe haven is purely interim.

These heroes speak the author's rejection of absolute values or final judgments—of even the supposedly eternal verities of simple literary critics. They cannot find truths because an impersonal universe without even pretended justice has forced them toward merely human unabsolutes. But to Vidal the adventure of the human condition is fit motive for living and writing. *The Judgment of Paris* and *Messiah* are strongly humanistic: Paris rejects worldly power and abstract knowledge for love, a recognizably brief but nevertheless valuable human love; and Eugene Luther knows, as he dies old, that life, not death, is meant to be the great adventure.

But a philosophy of relativity is not sufficiently rewarding materially to sustain life, and thereby sounds the second voice of Gore Vidal—the voice of the tradesman. Academics prefer to see their novelists pure and starved rather than tainted by getting and spending, especially if the getting has been munificent. Vidal chose a trade that bears grudging proximity to literature—that of mercenary dramatist. Twoscore television dramas, two Broadway successes (*Visit to a Small Planet* and *The Best Man*), and a half-dozen movie scripts sustained the abdicated novelist in the lean years of the mid-1950's. That the five-year planned piracy ended forever the bare bank account should not obscure the fact that Vidal did become a competent dramatist. The hidden cost exacted of him was, however, a compromising of standards: the manuscripts of the plays show that he has known a more bitter taste of the national dust than do the published or the acted versions. Yet the season of light satire did make it financially possible for Vidal the playwright to return to his calling, as his ninth and tenth novels—*Julian* and *Washington, D.C.*—demonstrated in 1964 and in 1967.

The third voice audible in Vidal's writing since *The City and the Pillar* appeared in 1948 speaks of a reasonable respect for homosexuality—a subject of national fascination but of critical cowardice. Jim Willard still moves in *The City and the Pillar* through the strata of our society: the small-town childhood, the athletic prowess, the sophisticated and the untutored pederasts whom he meets, his baffled search for love—all have made the protagonist into a small-scale folk hero. The point of *The City and the Pillar* and of those tender stories in *A Thirsty Evil* is that there should be no point, no pointed finger, and no fascination at all.

A fourth voice reflects another role which Vidal has played—that of the reasonable man in an unreasonable society. Just as the subject of homosexuality received a reasonable treatment in *The City and the Pillar*, so has he spoken on the emotional excesses of his nation. The essays collected in *Rocking the Boat* show a mind at work criticizing the national preoccupation with Love the Panacea, the right-wing political paranoia, the erosion of civil liberties, and the danger to writers in assuming that the cornucopia of mediocrity excuses mediocrity when guised as serious art. The civilized man must, as Vidal demonstrates, be mentor to his uncivilized brothers.

Finally, Vidal speaks as the voice of involvement to his age. A writer lives in his world of great unabsolutes and grubby human uncertainties; but he can, through the "understanding" that he so highly touts, be involved in shaping his nation, destined as it may be for cosmic nada. Vidal campaigned for Congress in 1960 and was (curious epithet!) an Almost Winner. He regularly contributes to the nation's merriment by speaking out on politics, owning a newspaper (*The Hyde Park Townsman*), and writing about politicians who are more successful in elections than he. He may yet be the first novelist to enliven the speeches made in Congress.

In all of these voices Gore Vidal speaks now, but it is as a writer that he should expect to be remembered. At the really unadvanced age of forty-two, with ten novels, four long dramas, and several dozen essays, short stories, and playlets published, what of the author's work is likely to be read in the next years?

There is *Williwaw,* the first novel. Vidal wrote the story of army sailors facing an Aleutian storm and their own conflicts when he was nineteen; but the clipped, understated prose still works. There is *The City and the Pillar,* destined to remain in print for the instruction of a fascinated nation. (However, the revised 1965 version will be the text.) There is *The Judgment of Paris,* Vidal's Peacock-like novel-as-dialogue, marred by only the young hero's opting for love. Finally, there are *Julian* and *Washington, D.C.*—novels that demonstrate that as late as 1967 hatred of the absolute and attraction for intellect at work still operate in Gore Vidal. Were the author and his ideas more deeply valued in the United States, that country would not need so desperately to hear his voices.

Notes and References

Notes and References

Chapter One

1. *Addison and Steele: Selections from The Tatler and The Spectator,* ed. Robert J. Allen (New York, 1957), p. 57.

2. Whenever a major work by Vidal is discussed at length in the critical chapters of this book, it is first documented there. The Bibliography, of course, lists all such works.

3. Kathleen Halton, "Interview with Gore Vidal," State Historical Society of Wisconsin MS, p. 10. Undocumented data in this chapter are drawn from the unpublished life records of Vidal deposited at the State Historical Society of Wisconsin (hereafter called SHSW). Such data are used through the permission of that Society and of Gore Vidal.

4. Eugene Walter, "Conversations with Gore Vidal," *Transatlantic Review,* No. 4 (Summer, 1960), p. 6.

5. Eve Auchincloss and Nancy Lynch, "Disturber of the Peace: Gore Vidal," *Mademoiselle,* LVIII (September, 1961), 179.

6. Letter, Gore Vidal to Ray White, June 14, 1966.

7. Walter, p. 6.

8. *Phillips Exeter Review,* X (Winter, 1943), 14-16.

9. *Ibid.,* X (Fall, 1942), 7-9.

10. *Ibid.,* X (Winter, 1943), 3-4.

11. *Three by Gore Vidal* (New York, 1962), p. 9.

12. *Ibid.*

13. *Ibid.,* p. 10.

14. Walter, p. 7.

15. *Three,* pp. 10-11.

16. Walter, p. 8.

17. *Rocking the Boat* (Boston, 1962), pp. xi-xii.

18. Walter, p. 11.

19. Auchincloss and Lynch, p. 179.

20. Walter, p. 11.

21. In *Visit to a Small Planet and Other Television Plays* (Boston, 1956), pp. 1-39.

22. *Ibid.,* pp. 127-72.

23. *Ibid.,* pp. 173-216.

24. *Ibid.,* pp. 217-33.

25. *Ibid.,* pp. 235-52.

26. *Ibid.,* pp. 253-78.

27. *Best Television Plays,* ed. Gore Vidal (New York, 1956).

28. "Television Drama, Circa 1956," *Theatre Arts,* XL (December, 1956), 85.

29. *Rocking the Boat,* p. 296.

30. Halton, p. 2.

31. Walter, pp. 16-17.

32. For Vidal's account of the emergence of writers into public life, see his "Writers in the Public Eye," *Times Literary Supplement,* November 25, 1965, pp. 1042-43.

33. Vidal's mother, Nina Gore Vidal, became the second wife of Hugh D. Auchincloss in 1935. In 1941, Jacqueline Bouvier Kennedy's mother became the third Mrs. Auchincloss. Mrs. Kennedy and Vidal are thus not related by blood. The relationship between President Kennedy and Vidal was moderately close; Vidal claims having suggested to Kennedy the idea for the Peace Corps. However, Vidal does not claim great admiration for Senator Robert Kennedy, against whose interests Vidal worked in the 1964 congressional elections in New York. See Vidal's "The Best Man: 1968," *Esquire,* LIX (March, 1963), 59-62; and his "The Holy Family," *Esquire,* LXVII (April, 1967), 99-102, 201-4. Vidal's best piece of political journalism, one that reveals much of his political thought, is his famous interview with Barry Goldwater, "A Liberal Meets Mr. Conservative," *Life,* L (June 9, 1961), 106, 108, 111-12, 114, 117-18; reprinted in *Rocking the Boat,* pp. 15-40.

34. Tom Prideaux, "A Family Heritage in Politics," *Life,* XLVIII (April 25, 1960), 60.

35. *Ibid.*

36. *Rocking the Boat,* p. 50.

37. *Ibid.,* p. xi.

38. *Ibid.,* pp. 58-59.

39. *Ibid.,* p. 288.

40. *Ibid.,* p. 58.

41. "Speaking of Books: Making and Remaking," *New York Times Book Review,* November 14, 1965, p. 2.

42. For an especially suspicious review of *The City and the Pillar Revised,* see Stephen Marcus, "A Second Look at Sodom," *New York Herald Tribune Book Week,* June 20, 1965, p. 5.

43. *Rocking the Boat,* pp. 289-90.

44. Auchincloss and Lynch, p. 133.

45. "Speech, late 1940's," SHSW MS, pp. 7-8.

46. Auchincloss and Lynch, p. 176.

47. Walter, p. 13.

48. *Rocking the Boat,* p. 140.

49. Halton, p. 14.

50. "Undated Speech," SHSW MS, p. 3.

51. Auchincloss and Lynch, p. 133.

52. "Speech, late 1940's," p. 6.

53. *Ibid.*, p. 1.

54. *Ibid.*

55. *Ibid.*, p. 2.

56. *Ibid.*, p. 4.

57. *Ibid.*, p. 3.

58. "Lecture of 1952," SHSW MS, p. 6.

59. "Speech, ca. 1955," SHSW MS, pp. 9-10.

60. *Rocking the Boat*, p. 137.

61. *Ibid.*, pp. 137-38.

62. First stated in "Speaking of Books," *New York Times Book Review*, August 5, 1956, p. 2. Reprinted in *Rocking the Boat*, pp. 147-50.

63. "The Role of the Writer in America" [*Esquire*'s Fourth National Literary Symposium], *Voices*, II, No. 3 (Spring, 1962), 19.

64. *Rocking the Boat*, p. 150.

65. *Ibid.*, p. 164.

Chapter Two

1. *Three*, p. 11. A remarkably good study of the genesis and development of this style is Richard Bridgman, *The Colloquial Style in America* (New York, 1966).

2. See A. T. Dickinson, Jr., *American Historical Fiction* (New York, 1963), pp. 208-30, for a list of one hundred ninety-four novels about World War II. This useful but incomplete list does not include Vidal's first novel.

3. New York, 1946.

4. *Three*, p. 11.

5. One World War II novel that closely resembles *Williwaw* in setting is Carl Jonas, *Beachhead on the Wind* (Boston, 1945), which describes salvage operations after a shipwreck on an Aleutian island.

6. *Three*, p. 10.

7. *Ibid.*, p. 11.

8. *Ibid.*

9. New York, 1947.

10. It is to be regretted that no writer or scholar—renowned or otherwise—has yet been daring enough to study the possible literary and social value and influence of recent American fiction dealing with homosexuality.

11. New York, 1948.

12. *The City and the Pillar Revised* (Boston, 1965), p. 245.

13. Walter, pp. 8-9.
14. Halton, p. 1.

Chapter Three

1. "Speech, ca. 1955," p. 6.
2. New York, 1949. Gore Vidal to Ray White, May 6, 1966: *"The Season of Comfort* is autobiographical which explains why it so perfectly fails."
3. *A Search for the King* (New York, 1950), p. 7.
4. One other American author, George Edward Rice, has used this subject. Rice's *Blondel: A Historic Fancy in Two Acts* (Boston, 1854) is most easily described as an "entertainment," a dramatic conglomeration featuring Robin Hood and his men, a love affair between Blondel and Maid Marian (!), and songs and dances set to contemporary melodies. For instance, the following amusing lines are to be sung by Blondel to the tune of "Stop dat Knocking at de Door":

> I've been, for some months, on a very dismal spree,—
> A king I'm acquainted with, I've tried in vain to see;
> If he is in the Castle, and hasn't gone to bed,
> I hope that at the window he'll show his royal head. (18)

5. Quoted in Oliver Evans, *The Ballad of Carson McCullers* (New York, 1966), p. 130.
6. New York, 1950.
7. New York, 1956.

Chapter Four

1. Fragment of a statement of personal philosophy, SHSW MS, p. 1.
2. *Ibid.*, p. 2.
3. New York, 1952.
4. *The Judgment of Paris* (New York, 1961), p. v.
5. New York, 1954.
6. Gore Vidal to Ray White, May 6, 1966.

Chapter Five

1. *Three Plays* (London, 1962), p. 253.
2. *Ibid.*
3. *Ibid.*, p. ix.
4. *Rocking the Boat*, p. 86.
5. Walter, p. 12.
6. Boston, 1957. Textual references are to *Three Plays*.

7. *Three Plays*, p. 259.
8. *Ibid.*, p. 258.
9. *Ibid.*, p. 259.
10. *Ibid.*
11. Boston, 1960. Textual references are to *Three Plays*.
12. *Three Plays*, p. 155.
13. *Ibid.*
14. *Ibid.*, p. 156.
15. *Ibid.*
16. *Rocking the Boat*, p. 300.
17. *Ibid.*, p. 299.
18. In *Three Plays*, pp. 87-150.
19. Not published. MS copy in SHSW.
20. *Three Plays*, p. 87.
21. *Ibid.*
22. "In the Shadow of the Scales," *Reporter*, XX (April 30, 1959), 40. Reprinted in *Rocking the Boat*, pp. 184-89.
23. *Romulus* (New York, 1966), p. x.
24. *Ibid.*, p. xiv.
25. *Ibid.*
26. Fragment of a statement of personal philosophy, p. 2.

Chapter Six

1. "The Best Man, Vintage 361, A.D.," *Life*, LVIII (June 12, 1964), 19.
2. Auchincloss and Lynch, p. 177.
3. Stebleton H. Nulle, "Julian and the Men of Letters," *Classical Journal*, LIV (March, 1959), 265. See also Nulle, "Julian *Redivivus*," *Centennial Review*, V (Summer, 1961), 320-38; and "Julian in America," *Classical Journal*, LXI (January, 1966), 165-75.
4. *Three*, p. 234.
5. "Self-interview I," SHSW MS, p. 2.
6. Boston, 1964.
7. "British Broadcasting Corporation Interview," SHSW MS, p. 4. Because literary critics would usually be less than at home in fourth-century history, I subjected *Julian* to comment from experts on the Emperor and his age. Walter Emil Kaegi of the University of Chicago writes: ". . . Vidal seems to have consulted many of the basic primary and secondary sources on Julian. He appears thoroughly familiar with the historical Julian, and he understands the fourth-century environment in which Julian lived and thought." (Walter Emil Kaegi to Ray White, September 18, 1965.)

Stebleton H. Nulle of Michigan State University remarks:

. . . I felt that Vidal had "got up" his subject very carefully, adhering to the evidence more closely than the run of historical novelists; and his inventions are well-contrived. . . . The simple fact is that no man of letters, here or abroad, has added anything to what we already know of Julian from his own rather considerable writings, or what we can get from his numerous biographers. His century was enormously confused: full of tensions and contradictions; and it would take a Toynbean range of learning, added to profound psychological insight, to give us more than an outward picture of this complex personality. . . . but who will recapture the spirit of the fourth century? In our anti-mystical, unmetaphysical age, no one is likely, then, to improve upon Vidal's *Julian.* (Stebleton H. Nulle to Ray White, January 28, 1966.)

8. "Self-interview II," SHSW MS, p. 9.
9. "Self-interview I," pp. 6-7.
10. "British Broadcasting Corporation Interview," p. 7.
11. "Self-interview I," p. 5.
12. "Self-interview II," p. 10.
13. "Self-interview I," p. 4.
14. Boston, 1967.
15. Gore Vidal to Ray White, March 23, 1967.
16. *Ibid.*

Chapter Seven

1. "Dirty Water," *Saturday Review of Literature,* XXIX (July 6, 1946), 27, 28.
2. "A. S.," "Aleutian Twister," *New York Times Book Review,* June 23, 1946, p. 4.
3. "A Strange Sort of War Casualty," *Saturday Review of Literature,* XXX (May 31, 1947), 21.
4. "Four Roads to Tomorrow," *New York Herald Tribune Weekly Book Review,* March 16, 1947, p. 10.
5. C. V. Terry, "The City and the Pillar," January 11, 1948, p. 22.
6. "Briefly Noted," XXIII (January 10, 1948), 81.
7. Richard B. Gehman, "Abnormal Doom," *New York Herald Tribune Weekly Book Review,* January 18, 1948, p. 6.
8. Richard McLaughlin, "Precarious States," XXXI (January 10, 1948), 14.
9. Philadelphia, 1948.
10. New York, 1948.

11. "Recent Phenomena," *Hudson Review,* I (Spring, 1948), 136-40.

12. Author's annotation to *The City and the Pillar,* SHSW copy.

13. "Mr. Vidal's Silver Cord," *New York Times Book Review,* February 6, 1949, p. 12.

14. "The Legend of Richard," *New York Times Book Review,* January 15, 1950, p. 16.

15. "Loveless Life, Banana Land," *New York Herald Tribune Book Review,* October 15, 1950, p. 10.

16. "Fiction," *Spectator,* CLXXXV (August 25, 1950), 252.

17. New York, 1951.

18. "The New Generation of Writers: With Some Reflections on the Older One," *Harper's,* CXCV (November, 1947), 423-32.

19. *Saturday Review of Literature,* XXXII (February 12, 1949), 6-8, 36-37, 42.

20. "A Boy and His Mom," *Saturday Review of Literature,* XXXII (January 15, 1949), 19-20.

21. P. 175.

22. Pp. 177-78.

23. P. 183. Aldridge has not changed his idea of Vidal's accomplishment. "I have not read *Julian,*" he writes, "but since my criticism of his work was based on the novels he wrote up through 1950 and should be considered to be my judgment of him as a young writer, I don't feel that any change is called for." (John Aldridge to Ray White, July 7, 1966.)

24. In the early 1950's, Vidal responded to Aldridge's criticism in *After the Lost Generation* with these words:

> John Aldridge in his interesting first novel *After the Lost Generation* depicts an imaginary world, set in present-day America and peopled with the names of such real if unlikely sounding people as Truman Capote, Tennessee Williams, and Gore Vidal who have all failed to reach the summit of literature not because of their youth but because they lack, in his pious words, values. Now I have since debated with him at Columbia and later at Princeton, egged on by Malcolm Cowley who supported my view and is therefore a good man, one in a million. To this day I have not got a clear declaration of values from Aldridge, or worse still, a definition of what he means by values and how their absence or presence helps or hinders literature. ("Speech, ca. 1955," SHSW MS, p. 8.)

At present, Vidal ruefully comments about Aldridge: "He is no longer taken seriously (not that he ever was, at least in those critical circles to which he aspired), but the danger he did in his day does live on, particularly in the Academy." (Gore Vidal to Ray White, February 22, 1965.)

25. Gore Vidal to Ray White, May 6, 1966.

26. "Seven Stories by Gore Vidal," *New York Herald Tribune Book Review*, February 17, 1957, p. 5.

27. William Peden, "On the Road to Self-Destruction," *New York Times Book Review*, January 27, 1957, p. 33.

28. Donald Malcolm, "At Home in a Gray Rubber Sack," CXXXVI (February 15, 1957), 20.

29. "Tension, Fun, and Faith," *Reporter* XVI (March 7, 1957), 40.

30. "Satire Comes to Broadway," *Reporter*, XXII (April 28, 1960), 38.

31. "Philosopher King—and Imperial Eagle Scout," *New York Herald Tribune Book Week*, June 7, 1964, p. 4.

32. "The Last Pagan," *New York Review of Books*, III (July 30, 1964), 21.

Selected Bibliography

Selected Bibliography

PRIMARY SOURCES

1. *Novels*

Williwaw. New York: E. P. Dutton and Company, Inc., 1946.
In a Yellow Wood. New York: E. P. Dutton and Company, Inc., 1947.
The City and the Pillar. New York: E. P. Dutton and Company, Inc., 1948.
The Season of Comfort. New York: E. P. Dutton and Company, Inc., 1949.
A Search for the King: A 12th Century Legend. New York: E. P. Dutton and Company, Inc., 1950.
Dark Green, Bright Red. New York: E. P. Dutton and Company, Inc., 1950.
The Judgment of Paris. New York: E. P. Dutton and Company, Inc., 1952. Revised edition; Boston: Little, Brown and Company, 1965.
Messiah. New York: E. P. Dutton and Company, Inc., 1954. Revised edition; Boston: Little, Brown and Company, 1965.
Julian. Boston: Little, Brown and Company, 1964.
The City and the Pillar Revised. Boston: Little, Brown and Company, 1965.
Washington, D.C. Boston: Little, Brown and Company, 1967.

2. *Short Stories*

A Thirsty Evil. New York: The Zero Press, 1956.

3. *Plays*

Visit to a Small Planet and Other Television Plays. Boston: Little, Brown and Company, 1956.
Visit to a Small Planet. Boston: Little, Brown and Company, 1957.
The Best Man: A Play about Politics. Boston: Little, Brown and Company, 1960.
Gore Vidal: Three Plays. London: William Heinemann, Ltd., 1962.
Romulus. New York: Grove Press, 1966.

4. *Essays*

Rocking the Boat. Boston: Little, Brown and Company, 1962.

5. *Other Volumes*

Best Television Plays. Edited by Gore Vidal. New York: Ballantine Books, 1956.

Three by Gore Vidal: Williwaw, A Thirsty Evil, Julian the Apostate.
New York: New American Library of World Literature, Inc.,
1962.

6. *Other Writings* (Exclusive of short stories collected in *A Thirsty
Evil,* essays collected in *Rocking the Boat,* and articles reprinted
in or from other volumes)

"Appointment with O'Hara," *New York Review of Books,* II (April
16, 1964), 5-7.

"The Best Man: 1968," *Esquire,* LIX (March, 1963), 59-62; ex-
cerpted in *U.S. News,* LVI (March 4, 1963), 19. .

"The Bride Wore a Business Suit," *Phillips Exeter Review,* X (Winter,
1943), 14-16.

"But Is It Legal?," *Partisan Review,* XXXII (Winter, 1965), 79-87.

"Byzantine Mozaic," *Reporter,* XXXIII (October 7, 1965), 54-57.

"Citizen Ken," *New York Review of Books,* I (December 12, 1963), 4.

"Comment: An Inside View on the Politician, and an Outside, or Porch
Slant, on the Teacher," *Esquire,* LVI (November, 1961), 202-4.

"Comment: Turn Left, or Right, to More Vivacious Matters," *Esquire,*
LVII (May, 1962), 159-62.

"E. Nesbit," *New York Review of Books,* III (December 3, 1964),
12-13.

"Five Poems," *Voices,* Summer, 1946, pp. 27-29.

"Indicting the Piper," *New York Herald Tribune Book Week,* November 3, 1963, p. 3.

"The Holy Family," *Esquire,* LXVII (April, 1967), 99-102, 201-4.

"Mostly About Geoffrey," *Phillips Exeter Review,* X (Fall, 1942), 7-9.

"New Year's Eve," *Phillips Exeter Review,* X (Winter, 1943), 3-4.

"The Novel in the Age of Science," *Quarterly Journal of the Library
of Congress,* October, 1965, 288-99.

"Oh, Henry," *New York Herald Tribune Book Week,* August 1, 1965,
pp. 1, 10.

"On Pornography," *New York Review of Books,* VI (March 31, 1966),
4-6, 10.

"A Passage to Egypt: A Sophisticated Traveler's Adventures and Observations in a Most Curious Country, a Middle Ground in the
Pax Frigida," *Esquire,* LVIII (October, 1962), 139-40, 142-44,
146, 148, 150, 152, 155, 156-57.

"Semisonnet," *Phillips Exeter Review,* IX (Spring, 1942), 14.

"Sir John, by a Nose," *Reporter,* XXI (October 15, 1959), 38-39.

"Speaking of Books: John Horne Burns," *New York Times Book Review,* May 30, 1965, pp. 2, 22.

"Speaking of Books: Making and Remaking," *New York Times Book
Review,* November 14, 1965, pp. 2, 82.

Selected Bibliography

"Tarzan Revisited," *Esquire*, LX (December, 1963), 192, 262-63.
"Tennessee Williams," *McCall's*, XCIV (October, 1966), 107.
"Three Minor Poets," *Voices*, Summer, 1956, pp. 46-48.
"To R. K. B.'s Lost Generation," *Phillips Exeter Review*, IX (Fall, 1941), 17.
"Tower of Stone," *Phillips Exeter Review*, IX (Fall, 1941), 24.
"Union Station," *Phillips Exeter Review*, X (Winter, 1943), 23.
"Vidal to Vidal: On Misusing the Past," *Harper's*, CCXXXI (October, 1965), 162-64.
"Writers in the Public Eye," *Times Literary Supplement*, November 25, 1965, pp. 1042-43.

SECONDARY SOURCES

Although Gore Vidal has never enjoyed an extensive press and although most criticism of his works has appeared in book reviews of little perception and slight value, the articles and reviews listed below form a selection of materials that should be interesting and useful to the reader of Vidal's fiction, plays, and essays.

ALDRIDGE, JOHN W. "America's Young Novelists: Uneasy Inheritors of a Revolution," *Saturday Review of Literature*, XXXII (February 12, 1949), 6-8, 36-37, 42. This critic, later to write so harshly of Vidal's early work, here expresses his admiration for *Williwaw* and *In a Yellow Wood*.
————. "A Boy and His Mom," *Saturday Review of Literature*, XXXII (January 15, 1949), 19-20. Aldridge overcomes his dislike of Vidal's fictional heroes enough to criticize *The Season of Comfort* for its structural failures.
————. "Gore Vidal: The Search for a King," *After the Lost Generation: A Critical Study of the Writers of Two Wars*. New York: McGraw, 1951. Still the most influential criticism of Vidal's novels, this critique of the early works cannot be ignored; but Aldridge's demand for absolute values in all fiction is scarcely acceptable.
————. "The New Generation of Writers: With Some Reflections on the Older Ones," *Harper's*, CXCV (November, 1947), 423-32. Develops the idea that the great writers of the 1920's are dead and praises Vidal's *In a Yellow Wood* as representative of the work of the new writers.
————. "Three Tempted Him," *New York Times Book Review*, March 9, 1952, pp. 4, 29. Considers *The Judgment of Paris* better than any of Vidal's early novels and hopes that the period of "apprenticeship" is over.

ALLEN, WALTER. "The Last Pagan," *New York Review of Books*, III (July 30, 1964), 20-21. Compares *Julian* to *The Judgment of Paris* in a strongly admiring review of *Julian*.

ASCOLI, MAX. "Satire Comes to Broadway," *Reporter*, XXII (April 28, 1960), 38-39. A sound discussion of *The Best Man;* appreciative of Vidal's political satire.

AUCHINCLOSS, EVE and NANCY LYNCH (eds.). "Disturber of the Peace: Gore Vidal," *Mademoiselle*, LVIII (September, 1961), 132-33, 176-77, 179. Especially valuable interview in which Vidal discusses marriage, sex, literature, his youth, and his personal preoccupations.

AUCHINCLOSS, LOUIS. "The Best Man, Vintage 361 A.D.," *Life*, LVIII (June 12, 1964), 19, 21. Develops the idea that the theme in Vidal's works is "power," as demonstrated in *Julian*.

BARKHAM, JOHN. "The Author," *Saturday Review*, XLVI (August 4, 1962), 19. Brief interview in which Vidal comments on the theater, revising novels, and politics.

BARR, DONALD. "From Patio to Jungle," *New York Times Book Review*, October 8, 1950, pp. 4, 28. A serious reading of *Dark Green, Bright Red* that finds little to admire.

BREIT, HARVEY. "A Talk with Gore Vidal," *New York Times Book Review*, January 22, 1950, p. 14. Early interview in which Vidal discusses contemporary criticism and sees the possibility of his becoming a satirist.

BROOKS, JOHN. "Fighting Somebody Else's Revolution," *Saturday Review of Literature*, XXXIII (October 14, 1950), 15. Comic reading of *Dark Green, Bright Red* that finds much to admire in the novel.

CHEATHAM, RICHARD. "A Visit to a Young Success," *Diplomat*, July, 1957, p. 22. Fawning praise for "a brilliant man."

CLURMAN, HAROLD. "Theatre," *Nation*, CXCIV (February 3, 1962), 106-7. Dislikes Vidal's corrupting Duerrenmatt's *Romulus der Grosse* with topical allusions and "aimless sophistication."

FITTS, DUDLEY. "Engaged in Life and in a Pagan Past," *New York Times Book Review*, May 31, 1964, p. 4. Admires the attempt at inclusiveness and depth in *Julian* but deplores the presentation of philosophy and theology.

GEISMAR, MAXWELL. "Deadly Altar," *New York Times Book Review*, April 25, 1954, p. 4. Admires the conception of Vidal's *Messiah* but criticizes its clinical attitude toward "reality."

"Gore Vidal," *Current Biography*, XXVI (February, 1965), 37-39. Valuable for concisely presenting the facts of Vidal's life.

"Gore Vidal: Politician," *Nation*, CXC (April 16, 1960), 326-27. Endorsement of Vidal's congressional candidacy.

Selected Bibliography

HARVEY, MARY KERSEY. "The Author," *Saturday Review*, XLVII (June 6, 1964), 32. Casual, not very informative interview with Vidal.

HAYES, RICHARD. "The Ministers without Portfolio," *Commonweal*, LXXII (April 29, 1960), 128-29. Applies the charge of "clinical sterility," so often aimed at Vidal's fiction, to *The Best Man*.

HEIMER, MEL. "Jack-of-all Crafts," *Pictorial TView*, June 2, 1957, p. 14. Vidal's need for money caused him to write drama for television.

HEWES, HENRY. "Sunny Side Down," *Saturday Review*, XLV (January 27, 1962), 29. Sympathetic review of *Romulus* by a critic who understands Vidal's purpose in adapting the play.

LINDSAY, JOHN V. "From JFK to Love Love Love," *New York Times Book Review*, August 12, 1962, p. 5. A liberal politician's praise for Vidal's sophisticated iconoclasm in *Rocking the Boat*.

McLAUGHLIN, RICHARD. "Precarious Status," *Saturday Review of Literature*, XXXI (January 10, 1948), 14-15. Soundest American review of *The City and the Pillar;* sensible and admiring.

MANNES, MARYA. "Tension, Fun, and Faith," *Reporter*, XVI (March 7, 1957), 40. Praises the satire in *Visit to a Small Planet* while admitting that the play is merely a group of humorous scenes.

MARCUS, STEPHEN. "A Second Look at Sodom," *New York Herald Tribune Book Week*, June 20, 1965, p. 5. Interesting review of Vidal's revision of *The City and the Pillar;* prefers the earlier, youthful version.

NULLE, STEBLETON H. "Julian and the Men of Letters," *Classical Journal*, LVI (March, 1959), 257-66. Excellent discussion of Julian as characterized by the world's great writers.

———. "Julian in America," *Classical Journal*, LXI (January, 1966), 165-75. On the Emperor as received in the United States.

———. "Julian *Redivivus*," *Centennial Review*, V (Spring, 1961), 320-38. Summary of Renaissance attitudes toward Julian; used by Vidal in his own research.

PEDEN, WILLIAM. "On the Road to Self-Destruction," *New York Times Book Review*, January 27, 1957, p. 33. Disparaging review of *A Thirsty Evil;* typical of the rabid mass-media reception assured any Vidal work dealing with homosexuality.

PRIDEAUX, TOM. "A Family Heritage in Politics," *Life*, XLVIII (April 25, 1960), 58, 60. Brief discussion of Vidal just before his congressional campaign.

"The Role of the Writer in America" [*Esquire's* Fourth National Literary Symposium], *Voices*, II, No. 3 (Spring, 1962), 5-27, *passim*. Transcriptions of remarks by Vance Bourjaily, William Styron, Nelson Algren, and Vidal, who discusses his theory that the novel has lost its public.

SHRIKE, J. S. "Recent Phenomena," *Hudson Review*, I (Spring, 1948), 136-38, 140, 142, 144. Discusses together Vidal's *The City and the Pillar*, Kinsey's *Sexual Behavior in the Human Male*, and Truman Capote's *Other Voices, Other Rooms;* likes the philosophizing of *The City and the Pillar* more than the story.

TERRY, C. V. "The City and the Pillar," *New York Times Book Review*, January 11, 1948, p. 22. Sees Vidal's novel as just another on a "groaning shelf" of works on homosexuality.

WAKEFIELD, D. "Gore Vidal: The Best Man," *Nation*, CXCI (October 8, 1960), 222-24. An expected, liberal endorsement of Vidal for Congress.

WALTER, EUGENE. "Conversations with Gore Vidal," *Transatlantic Review*, No. 4 (Summer, 1960), pp. 5-17. Valuable interview in which Vidal discusses his early novels, especially *The City and the Pillar*.

WARNER, REX. "Philosopher King—and Imperial Eagle Scout," *New York Herald Tribune Book Week*, June 7, 1964, p. 4. Considers *Julian* a flawed but interesting novel on the life of a flawed but interesting man.

WILLIAMS, TENNESSEE. "Gore Vidal," *McCall's*, XCIV (October, 1966), 107. Appreciative sketch by one of Vidal's closest friends.

Index

Index

Index

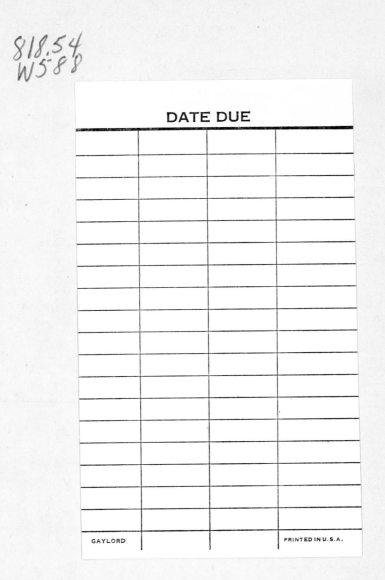

DATE DUE